MRS GROFF'S MISCHIEVOU
BOOK OF
MOTHERHOO
MANAGEME

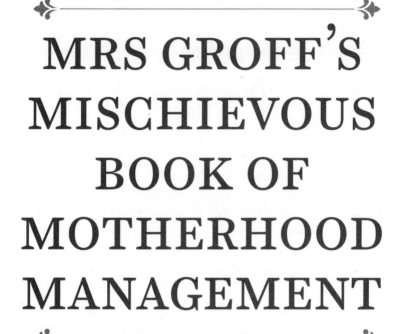

MRS GROFF'S MISCHIEVOUS BOOK OF MOTHERHOOD MANAGEMENT

Maggie Groff

BANTAM
SYDNEY AUCKLAND TORONTO NEW YORK LONDON

The information provided in this book is for general purposes only.
It is not intended as and should not be relied upon as medical advice.
A medical practitioner should be consulted if you have any concerns about
you, or your child's, health.

BANTAM
UK | USA | Canada | Ireland | Australia
India | New Zealand | South Africa | China

 Penguin
Random House
Australia

Bantam Australia is part of the Penguin Random House group of companies whose
addresses can be found at global.penguinrandomhouse.com.

First published by Bantam in 2019

Cover design and illustrations by Louisa Maggio © Penguin Random
House Australia Pty Ltd
Text design by Louisa Maggio © Penguin Random House Australia Pty Ltd
Typeset in 12/15.5 pt Adobe Caslon by Post Pre-press, Brisbane
Printed and bound in Australia by Griffin Press, part of Ovato, an accredited
ISO AS/NZS 14001 Environmental Management Systems printer

 A catalogue record for this
book is available from the
NATIONAL
LIBRARY National Library of Australia
OF AUSTRALIA

ISBN 978 0 14379 520 9

penguin.com.au

MIX
Paper from
responsible sources
FSC
www.fsc.org FSC® C009448

Contents

FOR MR GROFF,
light of my days, knight of my nights

Who is Mrs Groff?

Mrs Groff is the friend all mothers need. She knows things – important things like clever ways to lighten the mother-load, practical solutions that will save you time, how to fly around the world with an infant, and how to return to the workforce without going completely nuts. And she knows other things too, like how to host a birthday party and that tending to a baby is what's meant by life's ups and downs. Best of all, she smooths out bumps on the roadmap of modern motherhood, so dive into this sparkle of a book and get to know Mrs Groff. Like us, we think you'll love her.

Congratulations to us! We're 21st-century mothers who can and will pursue our own agendas, and no one, especially not our children, will control our destinies.

Oh ha, ha. Ha! HA! HA!

HA! HA! HA!
HA! HA!

ONE

Oh, Mother!

'Enjoy it, it goes so fast' refers to the moment of conception. Motherhood isn't going anywhere. It's for always.

FIVE THINGS MOTHERS DO EVERY DAY

1. Get up at least once while eating a meal.
2. Say, 'Don't do that!'
3. Sniff clothes to see if they will cope with one more wear.
4. Hold a conversation while sitting on the toilet.
5. Tell someone to wash their hands.

THE MOTHERHOOD ORGANISATION

It doesn't matter if you are a robotics engineer, a 3D artist, a police officer, a paediatric nurse, a personal assistant, a mathematics teacher, a commercial pilot, or even if you are not in the paid workforce at all, if you are a mother you are automatically a member of the best, the oldest, the largest and the most exclusive organisation in the world – in other words, the mother of all organisations.

So welcome to the tribe!

It has to be said that few of us were impressed with the initiation ceremony, and most of us have tummies that will never return to showroom condition, but we all agree on two important issues:

1. The first fifty years of motherhood are the hardest.
2. There is no such thing as a non-working mother.

DID YOU KNOW

DNA studies in Germany have shown that for much of human history there have been more mothers in the world than fathers. That's a win!

REVEALED: THE TRIALS OF OUR FOCUS GROUP

Like all major organisations, we have some members who live in cloud cuckoo-land and who are focused on themselves. You know the type. While the rest of us are keeping up with the laundry, they are keeping up with the Kardashians.

In between botox appointments and posing for selfies

in new yoga outfits, they worry that their housekeepers are not cleaning behind the furniture properly and that their offspring, Phoenix Princeton and Sierra Sunrise, have not yet been identified by their school teachers as gifted.

But no matter, we love their madness because it adds colourful fabric to the rich and glorious patchwork of mothers out there. After all, it isn't their fault that their brains fell out with the placentas.

P.S. I should also tell you that the majority of mothers, while still in the delivery room, promised themselves that their children would never eat fast food, never be bribed with treats to keep them quiet, never be allowed to play with their phones and never, absolutely never ever, be allowed to watch more than one hour of television a week.

And we all broke those promises by the third harvest moon.

❧ MEMO ❧

Admire and cherish your body because it is a wondrous work of art. It has made another human being. Nurture it, exercise it and give it the best chocolate. And remember, round is a figure too.

SEVEN SMART STRATEGIES FROM SUPER-SAVVY MOTHERS I INTERVIEWED ON A FERRY TO SYDNEY'S TARONGA ZOO

Listen to advice from other mothers. You have to, because they are going to give it to you whether you want to hear it or not.

◆

If you have to fire an arrow of truth at another mother, dip the point in kindness first.

✦

When someone pays you a compliment, don't deny it. Smile and thank them as if they have given you a gift, because they have.

✦

Be easygoing with yourself. Don't set targets that are difficult for you to live by.

✦

Don't lift anything over five kilos (about eleven pounds) unless it's crying.

✦

Rest when you can. The old adage that hard work never killed anyone is a blatant lie. Hard work has killed millions of mothers.

✦

It is absolutely okay to scream occasionally.

MOTHERS' MISSION STATEMENT

Ha! I bet you didn't know there was one, did you? But every good organisation has a mission statement to showcase their aims and values, and because mothers live in the real world, phrases like 'core competency', 'prescriptive evaluation' and 'differentiated objectives' have been dismissed as bewildering rubbish. Ditto 'blue-sky thinking', 'on the runway' and 'open the kimono' (an activity that introduced many of us to the organisation in the first place).

Our statement has to include all of us – the strong and the weak, the fat and the thin, the rich and the poor, the advantaged and the disadvantaged. And here it is:

To be the best mothers we can
with the situation we've been given.

DID YOU KNOW

Mothers gain automatic membership of a world's best-practice fitness organisation. Run by small and noisy 'in-house' personal trainers, the invigorating classes include daily stretching and bending with laundry aerobics, weight-training with living weights, power walking with the ever-popular stroller workout, marathon running after escapees, and everyone's favourite, an hour of core muscle-strengthening with a mop and vacuum cleaner.

INVALUABLE TIPS MY OWN MOTHER GAVE ME

1. Always marry money, darling.
2. Always choose new carpet with the colour of red wine already in it.
3. Always have cold cooked sausages in the fridge because men love them (sausages, not fridges).
4. The fresher the egg, the harder it is to peel.
5. Teenage boys have Ferrari-fuelled underpants.

(I didn't listen to any of it, particularly the last one.)

QUALITY TIME

Quality Time has nothing to do with children. Every mother in the land knows that Quality Time is being home alone with a good book or movie and a very large dessert.

REMEMBER: DESSERTS is STRESSED spelled backwards.

THE SHOCKING ORIGINAL MEANING OF THE PHRASE 'CHILDREN SHOULD BE SEEN AND NOT HEARD'

This old English proverb dating from the 15th century originally meant that young females should keep silent. That's right, only girls! As time passed it grew to mean that all children could be nearby, but mustn't speak unless they were spoken to.

A FREE TWO-PART INSURANCE POLICY
THAT REQUIRES EFFORT

If you take nothing else away from this book, please let it be these two things because they comprise your lifelong insurance policy.

1. Do pelvic floor exercises every day for the rest of your life, especially if you had a vaginal delivery. This will help protect you from prolapsed pelvic organs and stress incontinence as you grow older. Also known as Kegel exercises, pelvic floor exercises are discreet and only take a few minutes. I still do mine when stopped at traffic lights. Five years ago we moved to a town with only one set of traffic lights, so I always go that way even though it makes the trip longer. I can't tell you how many times my husband says, 'I don't know why you come this way, it takes longer and we always have to stop.' Usually I just look at him with a strange expression on my face.

2. Nurture and sustain your female friendships. I'll say that again! Nurture and sustain your female friendships.

✤ MEMO ✤
If you live with an impatient person and you are not ready to go out (because you helped get everyone else ready first), hide the car keys in a pot plant. This is the only valid reason for having pot plants.

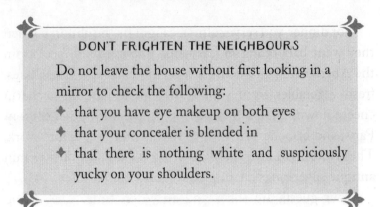

DON'T FRIGHTEN THE NEIGHBOURS

Do not leave the house without first looking in a mirror to check the following:

✦ that you have eye makeup on both eyes
✦ that your concealer is blended in
✦ that there is nothing white and suspiciously yucky on your shoulders.

THE DREAM VS THE REALITY

THE DREAM

There you go with your head in the air, a maternal superstar striding through the city in your pencil skirt and Jimmy Choo heels. You're an important person on your way to an important meeting, and you're leaving a jet stream of Chance by Chanel in your wake. You have already expressed breast milk for six-month-old Michaela Bingley-Bosworth, and instructed Julian, your latest PA, to call ahead and ensure that there will be camomile tea and figs marinating in spring water available for you in the boardroom. Julian, the treasure, is also organising a massage for you at 4 p.m.

Refreshed by an afternoon of fawning adulation from the suits at the meeting and the gentle rhythmic ministrations of Bruno's experienced hands, you arrive home and prepare an impromptu five-course dinner party for six visiting state dignitaries while feeding and bathing your seven children and fielding calls from your company's New York office.

For dinner, you serve salmon caught by the children when they went ballooning in Tasmania last weekend, beef from the Aberdeen Angus cattle station in which you have shares, fresh vegetables from your own organic garden, Vacherin cheese flown in from Switzerland, ripe Saturn peaches from Paris, and brioche that you made this morning before work. The white Irish linen napkins are pressed and rolled within antique silver rings bearing your family crest.

Your guests are sober and arrive on time. They bring burgundy from Domaine Leroy Chambertin. To set the tone, there is background music of you performing with Sting last year at Carnegie Hall. The food is sensational. The baby sleeps. At 7 p.m. on the dot your older children, who are wearing pyjamas that were hand-sewn by goat-herders in Nepal (part of your charitable foundation), perform Chopin's 'Nocturne' in B minor for the guests before saying good night in ten languages and happily retiring to bed.

The guests are impressed. *Une femme magnifique!* they say.

But your partner is on a one-way trip to the Lesser Antilles. And you haven't got any friends.

THE REALITY
You feed and polish the children before stepping into the shower. There is no soap. The phone rings, someone can't find their homework, another needs a gold coin for the cake stall, a tradesman arrives and the dog escapes. The children have opened the fridge and are suddenly wearing orange juice. And it's already 8 a.m.

By 9 a.m. you have dropped your children at school and are at the supermarket. You are buying chocolate biscuits and a cake for Julia at work's birthday morning tea. You don't even like Julia. You look down. You are wearing slippers. Maybe no one will notice. Back at the car, you glance in the mirror. You look like a person who needs lessons with Napoleon Perdis. Your stomach is rumbling because you missed breakfast. You tear open the chocolate biscuits and eat six.

Everyone at work notices the slippers. And the squashed banana on the back of your skirt. As an excuse for the slippers, you grab a bandage from the first aid box, remove both slippers and apply the bandage to one foot. To hide the stain on your skirt you twist it around so the stain is at the front, and then limp around carrying a strategically placed clipboard over the stain.

For lunch you finish the cake as you can't take a break because you are leaving early to take the children to ballet and chess club. The ballet shoes were not packed in the schoolbag and there are tears. But chess club goes without drama. Until a pawn to queen's knight goes up an opponent's left nostril.

At home, it's spag bol for dinner. Oh no! You have lamb mince, not beef. Maybe no one will notice. Especially after you burn it a bit while chatting to a friend on the phone. A neighbour appears at the kitchen doorway to return the key used by the tradesman. There is loud drumming coming from an upstairs bedroom. It stops suddenly and there is a piercing scream. You and the neighbour look up. A door slams and someone shouts, 'I hate you, you sick fuck.' You smile at the neighbour who quietly retreats.

It's dinnertime and you dish out the spag bol, heavily disguised under Mount Parmesan.

'I'm not eating that!' announces the youngest.

'It's your favourite,' you say encouragingly.

'Not when it tastes like dead ferret,' comes the reply.

So it's frozen pizza for dinner. With a mandatory apple for dessert.

It's over. They are fed and watered and supposedly in bed. You collapse on the sofa, which feels lumpy. That's because two apples are under one of the cushions. But hey, the TV and wine are yours until your partner arrives home from a late meeting. But not quite. Someone small appears in your field of vision. A Christopher Columbus project is due in tomorrow and hasn't been started yet.

Aaaaaaaaaaaaaaaaaaaaaaaaaaaaaaaaaaaaah!

A BRIEF REMINDER OF NANA NONSENSE

'Don't make faces or the wind will change and you'll stay that way.'

'Watching too much television will make your eyes square.'

'Finish that! There are starving children in Africa.'

'Burnt toast will make you pretty.'

'That'll put meat on your bones.'

'Shut the door. You weren't born in a barn.'

'Eat your crusts so your hair will curl.'

N.B. The toast thing doesn't work.

I'M HAVING A BABY!

Over the years there have been many euphemisms for pregnancy, from that elephantine gem 'great with child' to the doom-laden 'fallen' and 'in trouble'. Then we had the slightly more positive 'in the family way' and the ever popular 'expecting a happy event'. As time wore on things became more casual with eating for two, a bun in the oven, in the pudding club, knocked up, a bat in the cave and up the duff.

Surprisingly, at one time the word 'pregnant' was considered offensive. In 1952 when American comic Lucille Ball fought studio executives to have her real-life pregnancy written into her television series, she finally got her way but the word 'pregnant' was considered too vulgar to be used. In fact the executives were so scared Americans would be disgusted that the episode introducing Lucy's pregnancy was titled *Lucy is Enceinte* – using the French word for pregnant.

ATTENTION, MOTHERS, WE WERE HAD!

In his 1971 book *Bust-Up: The Uplifting Tale of Otto Titzling and the Development of the Bra*, the author Wallace Reyburn claimed the brassiere was invented by a man named Otto Titzling. The claim was widely accepted, even by the makers of the game Trivial Pursuit, and to this day, many people still believe it.

But it was a clever hoax. There are 4th-century murals depicting women wearing a cloth garment across their breasts, so the truth is that the idea of a bra, regardless of what the item was called, has been around for . . . well . . . centuries.

As for the innovator of the bra that we know today, the most money is on the French underwear queen Herminie Cadolle of Maison Cadolle in 1889, although many patents for brassieres were later granted to others across the globe.

THIS WOMAN CHANGED OUR LIVES AND MOST OF US DON'T EVEN KNOW HER NAME

Katharine McCormick (1875–1967) was a superstar of the women's movement and solely funded the research that developed the oral contraceptive pill.

McCormick was an American biologist, suffragist, philanthropist and a brave pioneer of women's birth control at a time when the very idea of women using contraception to prevent pregnancy was disapproved of.

In 1950 she was introduced to scientists Gregory Pincus and Min Chueh Chang at the Worcester Foundation for Experimental Biology in Shrewsbury, Massachusetts. Their work focused on developing a contraceptive pill, but they desperately needed money to continue and Katherine McCormick came to their rescue. She funded their research, which was obviously successful, and in 1960 the pill was licensed as an oral contraceptive by the US Food and Drug Administration.

A wonderfully eccentric woman, McCormick continued to fund major projects for women, and she was so pleased with the success of the contraceptive pill that she continued filling her own prescription for the pill well into her eighties – just because she could.

Katharine McCormick was responsible for the development of one of the greatest revolutions ever to happen in women's lives, namely allowing us to control our fertility independent of our partners, but her death at ninety-two went unnoticed in major international newspapers.

FIVE THINGS MOTHERS WANT

1. Larger print for dosage instructions on children's medicine bottles.

2. Disposable paper bras and/or undies to preserve our modesty in hospital when we have medical tests or investigations, unless there is a reason we have to be stark naked under the gown.

3. Restaurant seats that have a secure container for handbags built into the chair – under the seat pad, which is the lid.

4. For someone else to share the endless heavy load of our mental 'to do' lists so we can action our 'to be' lists.

5. Toilet paper within arm's reach of children in public toilets, not on the back of the door. Very funny. Not.

This will do for starters. More later . . .

GREAT GRAFFITI FROM ANCIENT ROME

Love it or hate it, graffiti is one of the world's oldest art forms. Ancient Romans freely expressed their opinions, comments, news and personal details in informative, frank, funny, crude and shocking ways by drawing and writing on city walls.

Fortunately for historians, volumes of their graffiti were preserved for all time when Mount Vesuvius erupted in 79 AD, burying the city of Pompeii in ash and pumice. Studied by scholars, these centuries-old words and sketches have provided valuable insight into life at that time. Most importantly, the words written by the mothers of Pompeii are about the only female voices recorded from so long ago.

Almost two thousand years ago, the following words (translated) were written on walls in Pompeii. I have added locations in case you visit:

Atimetus got me pregnant
(House of the Vibii merchants, Vicolo del Panettiere)

the man I am having dinner with is a barbarian
(the Basilica)

my lusty son, with how many women have you had sexual relations
(House of the Centenary, in the atrium)

vote for Lucius Popidius Sabinus. His grandmother worked so hard for his last election and is pleased with the results.
(on a city wall in Pompeii)

It's interesting how some graffiti continues to resonate. Many of us, for example, are still having dinner with a barbarian.

QUESTIONS, QUESTIONS, QUESTIONS

Once a child can talk, it's not an exaggeration to say that mothers are asked more questions every hour of every day than anyone else on the planet. Most of the time we are attentive and give proper answers, but on busy days when we are exhausted it's a total nightmare.

For years I've used one of the same four responses to any difficult question or statement delivered by children, teachers, neighbours, etc. The responses are polite, deflect conflict with confidence, and are an infallible first line of defence:

1. Thank you for letting me know.
2. We'll see.
3. Because I'm the mother.
4. What do you think?

TEST

Pick one of the above to match each of the following questions or statements:

1. Where do the people who live in our television do their wees?
2. Mum, why don't you have to sit in the back with the dog?
3. Can I have a Barbie Dreamhouse?
4. Daddy drove over the rose bush and said not to tell you.
5. Why do you get to have ice cream after I'm in bed?
6. Mrs McDonald, your child has been misbehaving in class again.
7. Who was the first mother's mother?
8. Natalie Rioli has a Barbie Dreamhouse.

WHO REALLY SAID THIS?

Most often attributed to the super-smart scientist Albert Einstein, but also to Benjamin Franklin and Mark Twain, there is a famous quote:

'Insanity is doing the same thing over and over again and expecting different results.'

Regardless of who said this, I don't think any of these men ever got children ready for school, do you?

KILLER BEAUTY TIPS FOR THE ABSOLUTELY EXHAUSTED

Don't go near your eyes with anything sharp.

✦

If you have swollen eyes in the morning from lack of sleep and chilled eye-pads aren't working for you, wet a cloth with hot tap water, wring it out and while sitting upright hold it over your eyes for about ninety seconds. Don't have it so hot that you burn yourself.

✦

If using concealer, dab it lightly onto blemishes and leave it for a minute before blending in with your fingertips.

✦

Invest in silk pillowcases. They don't leave marks on your face in the morning.

◆

Do not spray perfume on the front of your neck. This is thin skin and easily damaged. Spray or dab it on your inside wrist, behind your ears, and in your cleavage. My mother used to spray her perfume on all the pillows as well. She was quite territorial, my mother.

REMINDER FOR MOTHERS LIVING WITH FOURTEEN-YEAR-OLDS

Emptying the dishwasher is not for losers

A TWO-STEP TIP FOR MOTHERS WORKING FROM HOME

Trying to work with crawlers and toddlers around?
1. Buy a large playpen.
2. Set up your desk and a chair inside the playpen.
   Yes, the playpen is for you, not your child!

'I don't want to know what Grandma said about me,'
works every time.

PSYCHOLOGY IN ACTION

Tell a mother her baby is beautiful and she'll believe you.
Tell a mother her baby is intelligent and she'll believe you.
Tell a mother her child is gifted and she'll believe you.
But tell a mother a wall has wet paint and she'll touch it.

❖ MEMO ❖

The most important thing to understand about a two-year-old child is that you are both in love with the same person.

A SIMPLE SOLUTION TO A WEE PROBLEM!

Every so often flared pants or jeans with wider hems come back into fashion, and if you are wearing flat shoes or sandals you have to squat over a public toilet while trying to keep the hems of your jeans off the floor. An easy solution is to roll up the hems before entering the cubicle.

> ### REMINDER
>
> *As an aide-mémoire, if you don't use your phone for reminders, put a permanent dot on your toothbrush with nail varnish. When you clean your teeth last thing at night, seeing the dot should prompt you to remember something. It could be a reminder to make a tooth fairy delivery, take a pill, take something out of the freezer, pack a document in your work bag – or whatever.*

DO YOU KNOW THE REAL REASON WHY MOTHERS SHOULD WATCH THEIR OWN MOTHERS?

It's not to emulate them. It's because mothers will put up with all sorts of malaise without seeking help, and they do this for many reasons, which could include:

1. They don't wish to be a bother to anyone, especially their family and the doctor.

2. They fear the medical fraternity will dismiss their health complaints as being all in their head. Hey, it happens.
3. They fear they will be blamed for their symptoms and accused of not having had a better lifestyle, i.e. they should exercise more, they shouldn't eat sugar, they are overweight, etc.
4. They prefer to 'wait and see' if whatever ails them goes away.

So pay attention to your mother, and speak up if you think something is amiss.

A FRIGHT A DAY, IS IT? OH, YEAH!

There are two things you will start to notice when you become a mother that you never really paid attention to before.

1. Tabloid newspapers, magazines and websites regularly feature photographs of celebrities who have recently given birth. They are wearing bikinis and have returned to their pre-pregnancy shape in two days, or thereabouts. And their babies are nowhere in sight.

    You, on the other hand, are a normal woman who still has a tummy that resembles a partially inflated beach ball, and you are showcasing livid stretch marks that can be seen from the International Space Station. Personally speaking, I looked like a pineapple forced into a sock for about a year after giving birth – actually, I still do.

    The celebrities are usually lying on a yacht in Tahiti or looking glamorous on a beach in St Tropez, and they always have smug, sultry looks on their faces. In fact, they have exactly the sort of face you would never tire of slapping.

2. In the current global culture of blame you will also become aware that mothers, traditionally seen by many as soft targets, are often held responsible for everything that is wrong with anybody, and for anything that happens anywhere in the world. In fact teenagers, in-laws, teachers, politicians, lawyers and doctors point the finger at mothers so often that you have to wonder if it isn't some sort of tribal reflex.

The big end of town is also after us – particularly universities and institutes seeking funding for research, who regularly issue dire warnings such as (and I'm making this up) 'Overseas studies indicate that children of mothers who consumed dill pickles while pregnant are more likely to suffer acne in teenage years and have a reduced reading ability.' That sort of tosh.

Mothers are easy targets because we are mostly too busy or too tired to respond, but blame will keep being heaped upon us unless mothers take action. So try to respond to these annoying perpetrators, but keep it civil and don't use big words because that might confuse them.

N.B. If the dill pickle thing turns out to be true, remember you heard it here first.

❖ MEMO ❖

You can fool all of the children some of the time, and some of the children all the time, but with practice you will fool all the children all of the time. And their fathers.

REMINDER FOR WHEN YOU BECOME A MOTHER-IN-LAW

*Do not tell your son-in-law or daughter-in-law
how to bring up your grandchildren.
They live with your child and have seen your
previous efforts.*

IMPORTANT FREE ADVICE

ARE YOU USING THIS MAGIC BABYSITTING TIP?

It should be against the law for parents to have to prepare a meal for their children before going out to dinner, but it isn't.

There is an easy solution. Ask the babysitter to arrive an hour earlier and they can make the children's dinner and supervise the meal while you get ready to go out.

I know it adds to the cost, but it's money well spent.

HOW TO MARK YOUR TERRITORY

Yes. Males do it. Let's do it. Let's have mothers marking their territory.

Create a poster-size picture of yourself and the children and make sure you look glamorous.

Frame and hang the picture in your partner's workplace, right where their female workmates can see it.

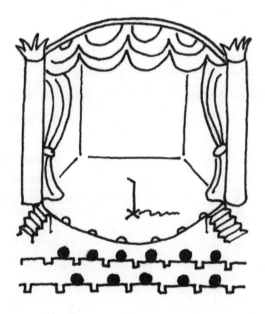

A tidy home, constant happiness, scholastic offspring, an obedient dog and scintillating family conversation at the dinner table are not real life. They are the prelude to a terrifying theatrical production that would give *Hamlet* and *Macbeth* a run for their money.

TWO

Hello New Mothers, Wherever You Are!

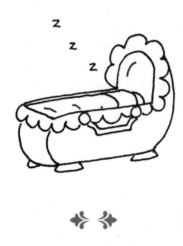

WAS YOUR BABY ON TIME?

A human mother's delivery date is calculated early in her pregnancy. It is assumed that women have twenty-eight-day menstrual cycles and ovulation occurs fourteen days into this cycle.

Your due date is the first day of your last menstrual period plus 280 days (forty weeks). As pregnancy occurs during ovulation, if you subtract the fourteen days from the total, this gives you 266 days (thirty-eight weeks), which is roughly the average human gestation.

However, according to some figures, only around 5 per cent of babies arrive on their due date. As we know.

*Tending to a new baby at night is what's meant
by life's little ups and downs.*

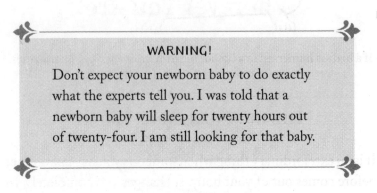

WARNING!

Don't expect your newborn baby to do exactly what the experts tell you. I was told that a newborn baby will sleep for twenty hours out of twenty-four. I am still looking for that baby.

❧ MEMO ❧

Trying to retain the lifestyle you had pre-motherhood is like pushing water uphill with a rake. It doesn't work too well. I was certain that I would easily incorporate my baby into normal everyday life, and I was adamant that no child of mine was going to dictate my existence. I even considered homeschooling. Just thinking about my naivety makes my head hurt all over.

THE NEW UNIMPROVED ARCHIMEDES PRINCIPLE

If a body is immersed in a liquid, the baby cries and your phone rings.

THE INCONCEIVABLE TRUTH

It is an extraordinary thing when someone you have never met before comes out of your body. It changes you completely. In that unforgettable moment of miraculous life, every woman instantly becomes vital, strong and fiercely protective. Her carefree, halcyon days of independence are over and she is now living for two people, one of whom is definitely in charge, and it isn't her.

At first, the new mother is shocked beyond belief and totally bewildered that her life is no longer her own. And she is completely unprepared for the overwhelming presence of her newfound maternal instinct, which is as powerful and drawing as gravity itself.

Women older and wiser have whispered to her that motherhood is the most challenging and most rewarding thing she will ever do, and that its life-affirming teachings have no parallel. And in that self-assured way of hers she had laughed, certain her previous challenges and achievements were higher, bigger, better. She had worked in New York and married in Venice. Climbed to base camp at Everest and canoed the Irrawaddy. Even hiked the Milford Track. She is certain the old ideas are no longer relevant to her global generation. She does not heed such antiquated thoughts about motherhood. But she does not know that those whispers have been passed down to every mother since Ancient Babylon. And for good reason. Because they are true.

In the euphoric early days she wonders why nobody mentioned that having a baby was like a wildly passionate love affair, unrelenting in its continuous power over her emotions. Or that when her child looks into her eyes, the outpouring of love and sensation of pure happiness is so strong it's tangible, and the high is so magnificent it is indescribable.

And then later, between daily labours of love and the seemingly endless grind of sleepless nights, the new mother secretly worries about everything, especially how she will cope. She is unaware that Mother Nature has her back, and that thousands of years of evolution have readied her mind and body for this experience by giving her incredible strength, intuition and capability, all of which will be there as and when she needs them. For the rest of her life.

Motherhood is nature at her best. And the wonders and rewards are like nothing else. You'll see.

❖ MEMO ❖

*Your maternal instinct will astonish you. No, you won't turn
into a sandal-wearing, tragic-voiced earthmother.
(Well, let's hope not.)
But take note of your reaction when someone mentions that
your precious diddums might have sticky-out ears.
That's the instinct we're looking for . . .*

RASPBERRIES TO A NEW BABY ROUTINE

You will receive plenty of free advice from well-meaning
people to quickly establish a new baby in a routine, but
ask yourself this: how can a living being who is growing
and changing their cellular makeup at the speed of sound
possibly have a routine? So don't panic – save the routine for
later, when you have settled into motherhood.

Honestly, for most mothers with a new baby, the fact that
Wednesday and Thursday follow Monday and Tuesday is as
close to routine as they'll get.

*No matter how hard you try not to,
you will turn into your own mother.*

HAVE YOU BEEN TOLD THE FOLLOWING GEM?

I lost count of the number of people who told me to lie down
every time my new baby slept. Right. And let the staff get on
with the chores.

Nevertheless, like an idiot, I decided to try it. And I remember planning a nap. It was a wet and windy day. No visitors. No appointments. Note on the door saying I was a lapsed member of two religions. My baby was asleep. What could possibly go wrong?

I lay down. A magpie flew into the window. Smack. Shatter. Thud. I spent the afternoon burying wildlife and phoning glass companies.

FIVE THINGS NEW MOTHERS WOULD LIKE

1. Really pretty underwear that is still practical for breastfeeding. For many of us, this is the first time we have ever had voluptuous bosoms and we don't want to wear pieces of construction engineering.

2. A good night's sleep. (Ha!)

3. A comfortable chair for breastfeeding at night, and warm slippers to wear if it's winter.

4. Someone to come in and clean our home, fridge, oven, windows, etc.

5. Another live-in helper at the beginning for a few days – either a relative or close friend.

'A mother's love for her child is like nothing else in the world. It knows no law, no pity. It dares all things and crushes down remorselessly all that stands in its path.'

Agatha Christie, mother and murder expert

SEVEN MORE STERLING TIPS FROM SUPER-SAVVY MOTHERS

1. If you're lucky enough to have her around, listen to your own mother's advice. Then do what you want.
2. Be lenient with your personal expectations. We are all amateurs when we sign up for first-time motherhood.
3. Don't waste this precious time trying to regiment your baby. Take things easy, and fit in with your baby's needs for a while until you have both found the middle ground.
4. You must be the mother you want to be. You are not performing for the approval of others.
5. Accept all help that is offered. And offer help when it is needed by other parents.
6. Never stand when you can sit, never sit when you can lie down, and never tell anyone you are doing either. Because if they see you, they will ask you to do something.
7. Enjoy your babies and children (in case no one else does).

TWO THINGS YOU MIGHT AS WELL ACCEPT NOW

1. Your lazy days at the beach are over. You are now on full alert at the beach (and the swimming pool) for the next twelve years.
2. You will have white stains on the shoulders of all your clothes for at least two years.

SAYONARA BREAKFAST

The only recognisable part of the word 'breakfast' for many new mothers is the 'fast' bit – either 'fast' as in 'go without' or 'fast' as in 'the speed of light'.

If a conventional breakfast isn't working and you need something in your stomach but don't have time to stop and sit down, try the following:

> As you move around, eat from a bowl of cut-up fruit that you prepared the night before. It's not ideal, but it will do.

> Make a banana smoothie. Combine a glass of milk, a banana, one tablespoon of malt and one tablespoon of honey in the blender and whizz it all together. Do this alone or you will be making them for everyone.

> Keep ready-made breakfast drinks or bars in the pantry for when you are really short of time and starving. If you are breastfeeding you must eat and drink something nourishing.

Have you ever wondered why you feel a certain way about something, but can't explain your reasons? Or have you ever sensed that you are being watched, and discovered that you are?

Here's why: in her infinite wisdom, and in order for the human race to survive, Mother Nature has blessed us with both maternal instinct and intuition.

Is there a difference between instinct and intuition? There sure is . . .

MOTHER NATURE IS OUR QUEEN, LISTEN TO HER.

INSTINCT

Instinct is our innate evolutionary and biological response to certain stimuli. We can't help it. It's not a feeling or anything that requires thought, but a primeval survival tool that ensures the future of our species. Instinct is one of the most powerful forces in nature. It is why a human baby, when it feels something against its cheek, will turn its head and latch onto the nipple and immediately suckle (we hope!). It's also why a breastfeeding mother's milk starts to flow when her baby cries (or when any baby cries, as it annoyingly was for me).

INTUITION

Intuition is like a sixth sense. An inner voice or gut feeling we have about something. It's how we sense we are being watched, and discover that we are. It's how we know when something isn't right. For example, it may be that we have reservations about leaving our baby with a certain person. Or feel there is something wrong with our child. We can't explain the thoughts and feelings. We can't rationalise them. We just know. And we are almost always right.

FOLLOW YOUR INSTINCT AND LISTEN TO YOUR INTUITION

Unfortunately, our daily lives have become so bombarded with information, instructions, advice and regulations that we have fallen out of the habit of listening and responding to our intuition. If you are concerned that there is something wrong with your child and, when you seek help, you are disbelieved or dismissed as being overprotective, then you must stand your ground and keep asking, shouting, whatever, until help is found and answers are given.

Mothers MUST listen to their intuition and trust it.

So now you know.

WHAT IS A LOTUS BIRTH?

Lotus birth is the term given to the practice of leaving the umbilical cord and placenta attached to the baby after delivery – i.e., not cutting the cord. The placenta is placed in a bag or bowl and carried around with the baby until the placenta and cord fall off at the baby's navel, usually after several days. It is rather a malodorous practice (as in smelly) but some mothers believe it is a more natural process and eases the baby's transition from the womb into the outside world.

Why is it called a 'lotus birth'? I flicked through my copy of Homer's *Odyssey* (that is encouragingly the same size as this book) for guidance but apart from the unwillingness of the lotus-eaters to leave their land, which could be seen as a placenta's decision to stay attached, Homer wasn't helpful.

So I'm going with the obvious. A lotus leaf is round and veiny with a stem coming from the middle and it looks like a placenta. But I could be wrong.

WHAT IS PLACENTOPHAGY?

Placentophagy is the practice of eating the placenta after the umbilical cord has been cut. It certainly isn't a dining option for me, but there are people who believe it provides health benefits to the mother. The placenta can be dried and made into capsules or put into a smoothie-type drink.

I'm actually feeling a little queasy now so I'll move on . . .

WHY DID THEY NAME THIS TOWN PLACENTIA?

The town of Placentia, California, is about a fifteen-minute drive from Disneyland. The name has nothing at all to do with childbirth and is said to derive from the Latin meaning 'pleasant place to live'. There is also a town called Placentia in the province of Newfoundland and Labrador, Canada.

As far as names go, Placentia is not as unusual as the towns that greet you in Pennsylvania when you drive through Blue Ball, Groffdale, Intercourse and Paradise, and then on up the road to meet your husband's family for the first time, where, on arrival, you can't stop laughing like a demented hyena. Been there. Done that.

A SMALL SPOTLIGHT ON OTHER
PLACENTA RITUALS

Whole books have been written on interesting things you can do with a placenta, and there are many cultures around the world that revere and honour the placenta for a broad range of reasons. Some wash it before burial, while others wash and anoint it with spices before a ceremonial internment. The Kwakiutl people of British Columbia bury a girl's placenta at high-water mark to ensure her skill at collecting clams, while a boy's placenta is left outside to be eaten by ravens and thereby ensure the boy has good vision. The Hopi Native American tribe of Arizona keep the placenta for twenty days and bury it after the ceremonial naming of the child. And the Baganda tribe in Uganda believe that the placenta is the child's double. The mother wraps the placenta in leaves and buries it under a palm tree, one species of tree for girls, another for boys. The palm tree is considered sacred and is fed the child's urine and faeces until the fruit is ripe. In New Zealand, the Maori people bury the placenta on the baby's ancestral land to establish a lifelong connection between the baby and their land. Some Native American tribes have similar traditions.

BREASTFEEDING

❖ MEMO ❖

*Breastfeeding is a triumph of natural engineering. I am
certain of this because the greatest scientists in the world
couldn't figure out how to turn beef casserole and lemon
meringue pie into milk, but my body could do it while
I was asleep. That's proof enough for me.*

WHO KNOWS

The World Health Organization (WHO) recommends that
all babies should be breastfed within the first hour after birth,
and then breastfed exclusively for the first six months of life.
Exclusive breastfeeding of babies under six months of age,
done a certain way, can act as a natural form of contraception,
although, as we know, nothing is foolproof. Known as the
Lactational Amenorrhea Method (LAM), the practice acts
to suppress ovulation – and you can't get pregnant if you don't
ovulate. Breastfeeding mothers wishing to do this should
seek advice from a breastfeeding specialist, as there are a few
simple conditions to adhere to.

CONFUSION ABOUNDS

In some English-speaking countries, particularly the United
States, expressions such as 'breastfeeding a baby' and 'nursing
a baby' mean exactly the same thing. In other countries such

as Australia and the United Kingdom, the term 'nursing a baby' simply means any person (not necessarily the mother) holding, cuddling, or rocking a baby.

MORE GUILT?

Almost all mothers want to breastfeed, but it can be very difficult for some mothers and their babies. Fortunately, there is help available from lactation specialists, baby health clinics, midwives, breastfeeding helplines and breastfeeding websites.

But what happens to the lovely and intelligent new mothers who have tried everything, but just can't do it? What then? Oh yes, now I remember, they are made to feel guilty and like failures by the Bosom Nazis, and their enjoyment of new motherhood is shattered.

If this is you, you are not a failure and you mustn't feel guilty. There are healthy, scientifically formulated milk substitutes available to feed your baby. And remember this – you have already given your baby thirty-eight weeks of nourishment, not to mention transferring antibodies and natural immunities, from your body.

So yes, you have fed your baby. And yes, you might feel sad that you are not able to breastfeed. But guilty and like a failure?

Never!

HERE ARE FIVE REASONS TO BREASTFEED

1. It's free, so breast milk is easy on the family budget.
2. It's portable, convenient and readily available, so there's no messing about with bottles and sterilisers.
3. It's a wonderful way to maintain the mother–baby bond, and it's also a regular sit-down for the mother.
4. Breast milk is always fresh and served at the right temperature.
5. It works on supply and demand – theoretically, the more milk your baby needs, the more milk your breasts will produce.

HERE ARE FIVE REASONS WHY SOME MOTHERS ARE NOT BREASTFEEDING (AND IT'S THEIR BUSINESS, NOT OURS)

There are valid reasons why a mother might not breastfeed, or is supplementing with formula. They might include:

1. The mother might want to have another baby as soon as possible and feels her chances of ovulating are higher if she doesn't breastfeed.
2. The mother's job (e.g. commercial airline pilot) and planned early return to work make it unfeasible.
3. The mother may be ill or on medications that contraindicate breastfeeding.
4. The mother may be undergoing chemotherapy or receiving radiation treatment.
5. The baby may have something wrong with its mouth and is unable to suckle.

So let's not judge each other, okay? Let's play nice.

THIS IS SURPRISING BUT TRUE

In a curiously ironic twist, the headquarters of the World Health Organization (which, as I've already said, recommends that babies should be breastfed for the first six months of life) is located in Avenue Appia, in Geneva, Switzerland, which is literally a healthy walk away from France, a country that has one of the lowest rates of breastfeeding in the developed world.

THIS IS TRUE BUT SURPRISING

In 1550 BC an Egyptian medical papyrus, the Papyrus Ebers, recommended the following:

'To get a supply of milk in a woman's breast for suckling a child, warm the bones of a swordfish in oil and rub her back with it.'

No comment from me on the validity of this claim, but I do have a picture in my mind of an old Egyptian medical man lying on the ground with a swordfish shoved down his throat.

HOW TO GO BACK TO SLEEP AFTER
A NIGHT-TIME FEED

It's easier if the baby is near you as you won't be actively over-stimulated from moving around too much.

❖

Don't speak. One word can break the somnolent spell. And tell your partner not to speak to you or ask you questions.

✦

Ignore suggestions about preparing cocoa in a thermos flask for you to drink in the night. Chocolate can keep you awake.

✦

Leave the classical music for cows in milking sheds.

✦

If you want, and if it helps you get back to sleep, feed your baby in bed. Check out the way to safely do this on a reputable breastfeeding website or ask your lactation specialist.

❖ BREASTFEEDING MEMO ❖

When changing sides while feeding, or if you need to stop during a feed, gently insert your little finger into your baby's mouth to break the seal.

CAN YOU HAVE A MASSAGE WHILE LACTATING?

Yes. It's great for relaxation and improving your circulation. As usual, keep your undies on, but you can also keep your bra on by unhooking it at the back and slipping your arms out, keeping breast pads in your bra to absorb any leakage.

It's normal to experience milk leakage during a massage. Advise your masseur that you are lactating and maybe place rolled towels above and below your breasts to stop any uncomfortable pressure. You can also express milk before-hand which might help reduce leakage.

DOWN THE TRACK, ARE YOU UP FOR THIS EXCITING REINVENTION?

When you wake up, don't speak to anyone or you will be asked to do something. And whatever you do, don't pick up your phone to check messages and emails.

Go straight to the shower and close the door. Wash, dress and do your hair without stopping. If there's time, slap on some lippy. It won't wear off, as you won't have time to eat until everyone else has gone, or the baby is back asleep. Short of head injury or flowing blood, ignore all attempts at interruption.

You are now ready for anything. Start the routine as soon as you can and don't waver. It will take a while for the household to stop sabotaging your intentions.

(N.B. You will not be able to do this until you have stopped breastfeeding. The baby must come first. Jump into the shower with full breasts and a crying baby and you'll have white fountains to rival those in Tivoli. Clever, but messy.)

MOTHER AND BABY MESSAGING

Mother and baby messaging is one of the world's oldest and simplest forms of communication. The baby cries to signal to their mother that they have a need, and the mother responds to the baby's signal by attending to that need, which is usually one of the following:

- hungry
- wet bottom or nappy rash
- unwell or in pain
- hot or cold
- want Mummy or Daddy
- bored
- frightened
- overtired.

WORRIED ABOUT THE NEIGHBOURS?

Remember that a crying baby sounds much louder to you than to others.

✦

Neighbours only get upset if a crying baby is left unattended.

✦

Bestow an occasional peace offering. A bottle of wine goes a long way.

✦

Given birth to the Glenn Miller Band? To absorb volume from the room, install heavy curtains, a rug, more furniture, cushions and a pile of towels.

WHAT IS THIS THING CALLED SLEEP?

I'm something of an expert on sleep – the lack of it, anyway. I blame heredity. My father, like Winston Churchill, only needed a few hours' kip a night. Me too. So, guess what I delivered one fine April morning? Yep. I got a female

Pavarotti. On the hour, every hour. For two years and eleven days. It wouldn't have mattered if she had been quiet, but no, that child was big on sharing.

I used to get wildly excited by books full of sleep tips for babies, and when the sun was at the right angle in our old apartment I could see the dent in the wall where I threw one of them (a book, not a baby). Nothing worked, and I tried it all.

Believe me, I was firm. But me and Miss Pavarotti, we just kept on with the nightly drama until that glorious day at the age of two years and eleven days when the opera rehearsals finished and she lay quietly in her cot. And oh, how this fat lady sang. But then I couldn't sleep at all because I was worried that my child was ill, or worse . . .

You see, for some of us, sleep ceases the moment we give birth and recommences once the dog dies and the children leave home. What happens in between is called *Nappus Interruptus*. And we just have to jolly well get on with it.

Chanting 'Rum Tum Tugger, Rum Tum Tugger,
go to sleep you little . . . darling' doesn't work. I tried it.

SLEEPING THROUGH?

Ah yes, those two magic words: 'sleeping through'. But what do they really mean?

For those mothers who have babies that are 'sleeping through' this mostly means from 11.30 p.m. to 4 a.m. To those who have babies that don't sleep through, in, over, under or beside anything, they think this means 7 p.m. to 7 a.m.

So please, shut up about your 'sleeping through' business. It just upsets the rest of us. I remember a mother at playgroup whose little darlings 'slept through' telling me that I had created the problem myself. She maintained this pious attitude until her third child arrived – oh my, how we all laughed then.

HOW TO PLAY MUSICAL BEDS

This is fun. Players start off in their own beds. By morning, the father is in the four-year-old's room and the mother, baby and seven-year-old are in the parental bed. The four-year-old is in the baby's cot. The dog is in the seven-year-old's bed.

And the little one says, 'Roll over, roll over . . .'

DESPERADO: LIKE 'DESIDERATA' BUT WITH NOBODY GOING PLACIDLY AMID THE NOISE

There are now so many people giving sleep advice about babies that it makes your head spin, but I can tell you that getting a tiny baby off to sleep – a tiny baby who doesn't want to go to sleep – is akin to completing an application form for NASA. I can also tell you the two things I learned, as follows:

1. Babies stay awake more each day as they get older. They can't do anything exciting until they are able to move around, so wake time involves being cooed at and cuddled, or lying in their cot staring at 4000 things you have stuck on the ceiling. Many babies drift off to sleep this way. Many don't.

2. Some babies lie in their cots and grizzle in a half-hearted fashion. Let them get on with it. Drop to the floor and crawl out of the room.

That's all very well but what do you do with twenty-odd inches of screaming, clench-fisted fury? Especially if you have a dreamboat who vomits if left to cry. You don't care if your baby is asleep or not. It's the crying that drives you up the wall, so you might pick one of the following systems and, if it works, stick to it like glue:

SYSTEM ONE
Pick up and cuddle your baby. Most babies settle when held upright with their head nestled in Mum's neck because this ensures she won't be able to do anything else. Walk around, sing and pat them gently on the bottom. Allow ten minutes after you think they have fallen asleep – they are tricky little devils – and then lay the baby down and continue singing and gently patting until you are certain they have nodded off. I could sing the complete lyrics of *Oklahoma!* to no effect.

SYSTEM TWO
Lay your baby in a pram or stroller, tuck them in and go for a walk (around the room is fine if it's night time). Motion is supposed to send a baby off to sleep. If it works, don't transfer them to a cot. It doesn't matter where they sleep, as long as they sleep.

SYSTEM THREE
Place them in their cot. Sit down, sing and pat the nappy area. If screams change to grizzle, get up and start tidying the room, occasionally giving a reassuring pat. Then creep out.

SYSTEM FOUR (FOR THE TRULY DESPERATE)
Put them in the car and go for a drive. Quite often, the whole performance can take three hours, by which time the baby needs feeding again. This is why new mothers say 'I never get anything done' and 'I don't remember'.

HOW I FAILED THE CONTROLLED CRYING TECHNIQUE

Controlled crying is recommended by many experts for babies over six months. There are several variations on the theme but essentially the technique teaches a baby to go to sleep on their own (can you see me smiling?). It involves letting the baby cry for a couple of minutes before giving basic comfort, such as a pat. You leave the room as soon as cries change to whimpers. Next, let them cry for five minutes, then return and repeat basic comfort, but leave as soon as screams subside. Repeat in increments of a few minutes until you reach a ten-minute maximum. You must be consistent for success.

I cried. I vomited. I failed. It was the most stressful thing I have ever done. Nature had not equipped me to go against my instinct – and my instinct was telling me that my baby was communicating with me in the only way she knew how, and that to ignore that communication would be wrong. Some people said I was sticking the proverbial rod up my own backside, so I wrote their names on a piece of paper and put the paper in the freezer.

WHERE IS THE BABY?

Not long after intercoms for babies' rooms came on the market I noticed that modern houses had developed an unusual floor plan. The 'main bedroom' (the term 'master bedroom' is no longer to be used) had turned into something called a 'parents' retreat', and it was located a long way from the children's rooms. It came with a pair of rollerskates for the mother.

Now, here's the rub. Your baby should be exactly where you want them to be – whether that's next to you in a bassinet or cot, or in a room down the hall.

And I'm not sure that everyone needs an intercom. Most mothers can hear their baby the other side of a pig shed.

BEDTIME FOR CHILDREN

You can lead a horse to water but you can't make it sleep . . . or something like that. But you know what I mean. Children need rest and sleep. They need routine. They need a seven o'clock deadline.

If children don't sleep well:

✦ They are bad tempered.

✦ They are unable to concentrate at school.

✦ Their immune system falters and they get sick.

Establish a routine and stick to it: toilet, bath, teeth, story and then bed. Leave the light on if they want, and give them a book, but after that, your job is done.

In some homes it's fashionable to keep children up so they can play with Mummy and/or Daddy when they get home from work. If it works for you, go for it, but I think Daddy should be playing with Mummy and vice versa.

Tired parents and tired children are a recipe for disaster.

DADDY (NO, WE HAVEN'T FORGOTTEN HIM)

Imagine this. It's a dark and stormy night. You're three months old, cold and hungry. Which would you prefer?

a) A soft-edged pinky vision with warm milky curves
or

b) A hairy man with rough scratchy skin who's using the f-word a lot?

Just asking . . .

HELP!

There are days when you reach the end of your tether and you need to sleep. Here's how to do it.

1. Ask a friend or relative for help during the day.

2. Feed your baby and hand them over to the helper. Tell them to go out for at least three hours or until the baby is hungry.
3. Put in earplugs and go to bed. Don't touch any housework.
4. When you wake, feed your baby again and hand them back.
5. Go back to bed for another three hours.

TWENTY GREAT GIFTS FOR A NEW MOTHER

(Many will also work for the baby shower.)

1. A four-week (or longer) subscription to a nappy service, if the mother has chosen to use cloth nappies.
2. A visit from a cleaning service one day a week for six weeks.
3. A day's help – the giver will do as they are told for eight hours.
4. A soft pashmina to drape across her neck and shoulders for night-time feeds.
5. A pair of top-quality yoga pants – so easy and comfortable.
6. *Mrs Groff's Mischievous Book of Motherhood Management*. (Ha!)
7. A scented room-diffuser to lighten the human aromas.
8. A flowering orchid in an attractive pot – the flower lasts for ages.
9. A voucher for a hair appointment, with the giver to babysit.
10. A voucher for a massage/beauty treatment, with the giver to babysit.
11. A basket of fragrant soaps and a fancy new shower cap.
12. A pair of soft, comfortable slippers for wearing at night-time feeds.
13. Top-quality hand cream – because lots of handwashing is going to happen.
14. For the baby shower, how about a beautiful pre-birth painting on the pregnant tummy? Check out belly painting available near you.

15. A children's birthday-cake cookbook. This will have many years of use.
16. A silver photo-frame (with a photo of the baby, if gifted after the birth).
17. A silver pendant of the baby's birthstone (Although this could be expensive, depending on the month).
18. Muslin squares – they're handy for protecting clothing, discreet feeding, spills, etc.
19. Seven days' supply of ready-made frozen meals, with sufficient portion sizes for all family members (always buy top quality). This may seem like an unexciting gift, but it will be really useful.
20. A coupon book (see below).

HOW TO MAKE A COUPON BOOK

This is the ideal present for a group of friends to prepare for a new mother. To compile one, have each person write a favour (handwritten is more personal) on a small sheet of paper.

Suggestions:

+ four hours' free babysitting on a Saturday night
+ one load of ironing
+ a day's help at home
+ one mow of the lawn
+ a trip to the movies plus babysitting.

Staple the coupons together and make a fancy front cover. It beats six rattles and four sets of bibs hands down.

NEW MOTHERS AND ESTABLISHING NEW FAMILY TRADITIONS

A word of caution: when you start a family, it's popular for new mothers to make a commitment to a new family tradition. It's one of those things that sounds like a good idea at the time, but isn't. You will set yourself up to fail if you commit to open-house for extended family on Sundays, night walks for your family every full moon, or announce that you will be having Halloween celebrations at your house every year because you're worried about children knocking on doors for treats.

If you think about it, the best family traditions – the ones that provide a sense of place and belonging – are those that have developed over time, like camping at the same beach with other families in summer, or a BBQ at your place every Grand Final day.

Maybe it's best, for now, to stick with simple customs you and your partner have inherited from your own families and allow your own traditions to be discovered over the years.

If you are still keen, even after I've pooped on the idea, the internet provides oodles of inspiration, but go for quality not quantity. There are many sweet ideas, but some are page-fillers – by which I mean activities you will do anyway, like reading to your child before bedtime, kissing them good-night, watching a family movie together every Wednesday, or having Sunday night pizza.

Don't forget to keep a national newspaper printed on the day your baby is born.

MAKING MEMORIES

Start a Memory Box for notes of your child's first words or funny things they say (it's easy to scribble a note and toss it in the box), their first shoes, small treasures they make for Mother's Day, their first drawing, painting, story, etc. You can collate it all later . . . let's say in about twenty years.

◆

Each birthday:
- Measure your child against the kitchen wall and mark their name and age in pencil. This visible graffiti marking announces that your child is more important to you than your house and it gives you an envy-inducing bohemian air. (N.B. Pencil marks can be rubbed off if you move.)
- Photograph your child outside the front door of where you live. Annual photos are great for their twenty-first birthday party.
- Write a letter to your child and keep it safe. The collection makes a wonderful twenty-first birthday present.

◆

Everyone needs a reason to buy Christmas tree decorations and here is yours – each year buy a special ornament and discreetly write your child's name and age on it somewhere. Apart from future Christmas fun where siblings are squabbling over who owns what, when they grow up and hopefully leave home they will have a collection of memories for their own trees.

✦

Save all school projects, as you will need them again – either for reference, or as emergency back-up material to crib from when the next–in–line informs you at 7 p.m. on a Sunday night that a project he hasn't done is due in tomorrow.

THREE

Troubleshooting for Mothers

TOP FIVE KILLER TRUTHS ABOUT
A CHILD'S BEHAVIOUR

1. Everyone else knows how to bring up and discipline your children much better than you do. Especially those with no children.
2. Children behave badly when they are hungry and tired, and reprimands inflame the situation.
3. Your response to bad behaviour is directly related to your location, other humans present, your tiredness and what is happening for the rest of the day. It rarely has anything to do with the level of naughtiness.
4. Children are naughty on windy days. Ask any schoolteacher.
5. Rewards hold more power than threats.

Remember, you are the grown-up. Copy this sign and paste it on the kitchen wall, especially if you have toddlers.

I
AM
THE
GROWN-UP!

LEARN THE BASTARD TECHNIQUE

Don't waste time trying to teach a lesson to a tired, hungry child who is misbehaving. Feed them and put them to bed. For damage control of misdemeanours and tantrums at other times, try using the BASTARD technique. It's simple. Occasionally it works.

BE SAFE. Remove the child from harm's way.
ANGER. Control yours.
SEPARATE the child from others.
TELL the child you are upset and why.
APPROPRIATE punishment. Choose one and follow through.
REPAIR. Make the child apologise.
DRINK. Chilled Chardonnay should make you feel better.

AN OFTEN-OVERLOOKED SIMPLE REMEDY TO A COMMON PREDICAMENT

PROBLEM: You have an important appointment in half an hour and your child is refusing to sit in the car seat.

ACTION: Don't lose your temper and never lose sight of the desired result, which is to be on time for the appointment and to be calm when you get there. Use whatever bribes or treats you have cunningly concealed in the glove compartment for exactly this occasion. Remember, this is your life too. Save the behaviour lesson for later.

✤ MEMO ✤
Smacking is bad ju-ju.

LOST IN A DEPARTMENT STORE

If your child is one of life's explorers who wander off in a large store or shopping centre, it might be a good idea to pin your name and phone number on them.

I have a friend who wishes she had labelled her three-year-old son before he suddenly took off from the change room in a department store while she was trying on a dress.

As my friend frantically searched the ladies fashion level in an unzipped cocktail dress, an announcement came over the store loudspeaker system: 'We have a little boy in the store looking for his mummy. His name is Poppet and his mummy is old and has big legs and none of the dresses here fit her.'

SEVEN TIPS FOR WHEN OPCs (OTHER PEOPLE'S CHILDREN) ARE NAUGHTY IN YOUR HOME

(This is a great subject for group discussion with wine.)

1. Banishing a revolting OPC from your home forever doesn't work. Someone will let them back in when they are fourteen and they will put a mouse in your makeup bag.
2. Remember that you are in charge and you are the grown-up.
3. Never strongly reprimand an OPC.
4. You must be seen by other children to be dealing with the situation.
5. Implement the BASTARD technique immediately (see page 56).
6. The appropriate punishment is that you will tell their parents what they have done. Nothing more.
7. Never assume your own child wouldn't behave badly in someone else's home. So be nice when you tell the OPC's parents. Just in case.

❖ IMPORTANT MEMO FOR CHILDREN ❖
Do not let your mother brush your hair if she is cross with you.

SLEEPWALKING

This strange behaviour tends to run in families. Young sleepwalkers often take to the boards not long after falling asleep. This allows for a certain measure of safety, as the activity occurs while you are still up and can protect them. Sometimes it's hard to tell they are asleep as their eyes are often open.

Safety is paramount if you live with a sleepwalker. Make sure you:

Secure bedroom windows and lock outside doors.

✦

Sew bells on the child's pyjamas and/or alarm their bedroom door by hanging an old fashioned bell from the ceiling so it will clang if the door is opened.

✦

Place a security gate at the top of the stairs.

It isn't necessary to wake sleepwalkers. Take them by the hand and lead them straight back to bed. And I wouldn't believe that nonsense about children growing out of it if I were you.

✦ MEMO ✦

The pain-relief properties of an ordinary bandaid are never to be questioned.

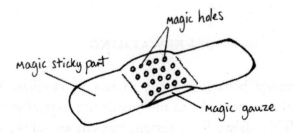

magic holes

magic sticky part

magic gauze

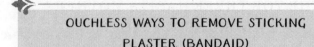

OUCHLESS WAYS TO REMOVE STICKING PLASTER (BANDAID)

Soak it off in the bath

or

cover with olive oil or baby oil and leave it to soak in. Then gently peel the plaster off. This also works with WD-40, but it's a bit smelly.

HOW TO REMOVE HEM MARKS

If you want to let down a dress, long pants or shorts, you'll need to remove the hem mark.

Make a solution of one cup (250 ml) hot water, half a teaspoon of white vinegar and a quarter of a teaspoon of borax. Mix well.

✦

Saturate a clean cloth in the solution.

✦

Wring out and lay the cloth over hem mark on the wrong side.

✦

Steam iron until cloth is dry.

✦

Brush hem when dry.

THE TOP THREE HABITS MOTHERS WORRY ABOUT MOST

1. THUMB-SUCKING

Thumb-sucking is both a comfort and a habit. Some babies start early and suck their thumbs in their mother's womb. It's basically harmless, but if continued for years it may damage teeth or the thumbnail.

TIP

Social pressure usually stops thumb-sucking, but don't worry too much about it. Look around. Do you see any adults still sucking their thumbs? Thought not.

2. NOSE-PICKING a.k.a. NASAL MINING

This is an unpleasant habit that can get out of hand. Nose-pickers are teased and can develop scabs around their nostrils.

TIPS

Teach the child it is revolting to see and should be done in private with a tissue.

When they pick, appeal to their sense of pride by saying, 'That looks awful,' rather than, 'Don't do that.'

Cut nails short to avoid nasal damage and give rewards for long periods of non-picking. Hopefully the child will stop picking in front of you. Slowly, short periods of abstinence should lengthen and the child will stop picking in front of other people as well.

3. NAIL-BITING

Nail-biting is common. It is not a sign of bad diet, but it is unpleasant to look at and can introduce nasty bugs into the mouth. You can do a lot to stop this habit, starting by keeping a child's nails short and tidy. Often, nail-biting begins with nibbling a sharp bit and hey presto, a habit develops.

TIPS

Cut nails once a week and file down tempting bits of nail that stick out.

✦

If nails are already nibbled, check daily and clip off any sharp bits.

✦

Purchase a specially formulated product for nail-biters from a pharmacy. It's painted on nails, is harmless and has an unpleasant taste. (On the upside this will make your cooking seem more delicious.)

✦

Pin a poster of the armless Venus de Milo on the child's bedroom wall. Tell them Venus was the Ancient Greek Nail-Biting Champion.

CRAZY OLD BELIEFS ABOUT THUMB-SUCKING THAT HAVE CAUSED DISTRESS

1. Sigmund Freud, father of psychoanalysis, wrote in 1905 that thumb-sucking caused masturbation, which was at the time considered a disease.
2. From the late 1870s to the early 1900s, thumb-sucking was classified by doctors as a neurological disease, to be treated by specialist paediatricians. Victorian parents hoped for a cure by tying their infant's arms by their sides at night.
3. Another radical solution to the scourge of innocent thumb-sucking was for mothers to read aloud to their children 'The Story of the Thumb-Sucker' from *Der Struwwelpeter* by Heinrich Hoffman (1845). In this delightful and heartwarming children's tale, the red-legged scissorman cuts off the thumb-suckers' thumbs with a large pair of scissors. The book's illustrations are the stuff of nightmares.

THE SEVEN MOST ANNOYING HABITS OF COMPLETELY NORMAL CHILDREN

1. fake vomiting and farting
2. exaggerated sighing
3. hair-twirling
4. sniffing
5. rolling eyes
6. making unattractive facial expressions
7. sticking out their tongue.

These habits usually start in imitation of a friend or classmate, and should last only a few days or weeks. You can either ignore the habit and it may go away, try explaining that such behaviour is not pleasant and they shouldn't do it, or respond in anger and the child will keep doing it. Your choice.

NIGHTMARES

Nightmares do no harm and they come and go through childhood like spring tides. If your child wakes screaming or in tears, go to them immediately. Hold them gently and whisper something soothing until they have fallen back asleep.

NIGHT TERRORS

Night terrors are far more frightening than nightmares. The child will wake and scream hysterically, and when you go to them they thrash out at you. There is usually a look of abject fear on their face.

A night terror is not a nightmare fantasy where a tiger is about to eat you up. It is a genuine emotional replay of real fear experienced from having been lost, or perhaps a stay in hospital where fear was compounded with pain.

Turn on the light, wake the child fully and go through the bedtime ritual again, for they will be too scared to go straight back to sleep. You will, too.

If night terrors continue you should seek professional help.

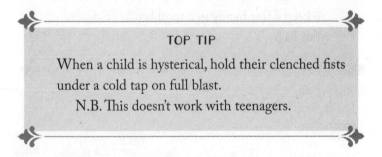

TOP TIP
When a child is hysterical, hold their clenched fists under a cold tap on full blast.

N.B. This doesn't work with teenagers.

WET BEDS

Having failed miserably in the sleeping baby department, I was immensely proud that I never had to change a child's wet bed, and frequently reminded friends with sleeping babies of this fact when they bemoaned changing wet beds in the night. I can hear them now saying, 'Oh, do shut up, Maggie.' So I shut up and listened, and this is what little I learned.

1. Place a second protector and bottom sheet over the existing ones so you have multiple layers and can take off the top wet sheet and protector and don't have to remake the whole bed at 3 a.m.

2. Male bed-wetters often soak the top bedding as well as the bottom sheet. Instead of a top sheet try using a good-quality soft nylon shower curtain to protect blankets.

SAVE THE STRAWS

Because of environmental concerns, many cafes and restaurants have stopped providing straws. But small children sometimes need a straw and there is nothing wrong with re-usable paper-based straws, so keep a few handy in a toothbrush holder in your bag.

HOW TO BANISH MONSTERS

A monster under the bed is a great excuse to have parents dashing in and out of the bedroom like demented fools. You will never have peace until you get rid of the monster.

BEST-PRACTICE MONSTER REMOVAL

1. During the night, trap the monster in an empty shoebox.
2. Let the child see you tie the shoebox with string and put it in the car ready for their father (or someone else) to drive it to the nearest river, where it will be released.
3. On their return, show the child the empty shoebox.

You're not really sure how far away the driver drove, are you? Well, that's exactly how it is with monsters. You can never know for sure.

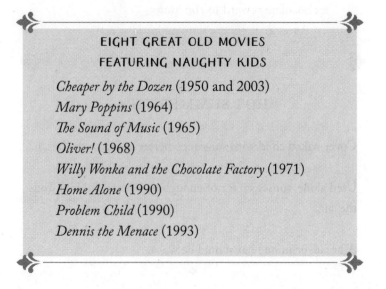

EIGHT GREAT OLD MOVIES
FEATURING NAUGHTY KIDS

Cheaper by the Dozen (1950 and 2003)

Mary Poppins (1964)

The Sound of Music (1965)

Oliver! (1968)

Willy Wonka and the Chocolate Factory (1971)

Home Alone (1990)

Problem Child (1990)

Dennis the Menace (1993)

HELP!

When a child has swallowed something odd you will need to contact help quickly, so make sure you know how to call your nearest Poisons Information Centre. The World Health Organization has a world directory of poison centres: apps.who.int/poisoncentres/.

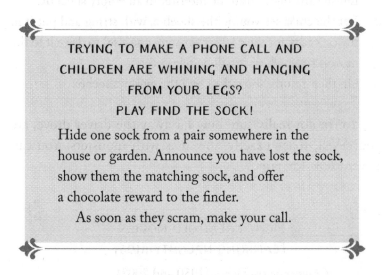

TRYING TO MAKE A PHONE CALL AND CHILDREN ARE WHINING AND HANGING FROM YOUR LEGS?
PLAY FIND THE SOCK!

Hide one sock from a pair somewhere in the house or garden. Announce you have lost the sock, show them the matching sock, and offer a chocolate reward to the finder.
As soon as they scram, make your call.

HOT SUMMER TIPS

Cover naked child with sunscreen before going to the beach.

Used alone, sunscreen is not enough to protect children from the sun.

A broad-brimmed hat should be worn.

Don't go to the beach during the hottest part of the day.

✦

Clouds don't stop sunburn.

✦

Closely woven fabrics provide the best protection.

✦

Light-coloured and white clothes reflect heat.

✦

Natural fibres (cotton) are the most comfortable.

✦

A collar protects the neck.

✦

Long-sleeved swim tops (rash vests) that are specially made for the beach and are marked 'SPF' provide good protection. SPF stands for Sun Protection Factor. It is a laboratory measure where an attempt is made to grade the product's ability to filter out UVB light.

✦

Children should wear sunglasses when outside in sunshine. Proper ones. Elastic can be attached to ends to hold them on.

✦

Children's scalps burn easily at the beach. Beware.

✦

If your child needs ear plugs for swimming but has lost them, at a pinch you can use a lump of Blu Tack instead, but don't push it in too far.

✦

A cool shower before bedtime will calm itchy skin and bites.

✦

On really hot nights, put sheets in a plastic bag in the fridge for a few hours before bedtime. Cool sheets are also helpful for itchy, bothered little sleepers.

BEWARE!

1. Surf and shallow water are dangerous. Don't let children, teenagers (or anyone) run into the surf and dive into a wave in shallow water. This is one of the causes of spinal injury.

2. Teach children never to jump into any still water unless they know how deep it is.

3. Never assume another adult, lifeguard or sibling is watching your young child at the beach or pool. It is your responsibility.

DO YOU KNOW THESE TWO SNEAKY WAYS TO ELICIT INFORMATION FROM A CHILD?

1. Ask your question and then remain silent, i.e. don't fill the air with anything. Children can't stand the silence and have to fill it with something – often the answer.

2. Firmly say, 'I don't want to know what Dad did while I was out.' Usually children can't help themselves and blurt it out. This method can work for years.

CONSERVATION AND THE ENVIRONMENT: A MODERN MOTHER'S DILEMMA

One day, when you are least expecting it, your child will call you a whale-murdering monster. It doesn't matter that you have never owned a coat made from the skin of a rare snow leopard, never roasted an endangered species for dinner, never built a holiday home on the edge of a Borneo rainforest, never stomped about in clogs on a coral reef, never spent a day at the beach throwing straws and plastic bags into the sea, and never harpooned a whale and motored about the bay with its bloody carcass tied to your dinghy, young Darwin will have been told that humans are destroying the planet, AND THAT MEANS YOU.

EMERGENCY RESPONSE
Blame everyone else, especially the government. And Cruella de Vil.

DAMAGE CONTROL
Focus on REDUCE and RE-USE and explain to the child what you already might be doing for the environment:

Reduce power usage by installing solar panels on the roof.

✦

Reduce water usage by installing rainwater tanks.

✦

Reduce power usage by harnessing solar and wind power to dry clothes outside.

✦

Reduce water usage by turning off taps while cleaning teeth, having children share baths, using water-level controls on the washing machine, and only running the dishwasher when it's full.

✦

Reduce landfill by recycling paper, plastic and glass.

✦

Reduce destruction of trees by not printing bills and emails.

✦

Reduce use of heating and air-conditioning by wearing cardigans and using windows for climate control.

✦

Reduce power usage by turning off lights when not in a room, and switching off equipment at wall sockets and not leaving things on stand-by.

✦

Take re-usable bags when grocery shopping.

✦

Re-use wrapping paper for birthdays and Christmas.

✦

Re-use children's clothing by sharing hand-me-downs.

✦

Re-use food scraps and reduce waste by using a compost bin to make natural fertiliser for the garden.

Ask your budding conservationist to consider:

Walking to and from school.

✦

Starting a worm farm (they will be excited by this).

✦

Donating their birthday money to a wildlife fund. (Watch your child go mad for this one. Hopefully they will be running away so fast they will forget about the worm farm.)

RESULTS

You have planted the seeds of REDUCE and RE-USE in your child's mind, and the whale-murdering monster is now a planet-saving princess. All is well.

DO YOU KNOW HAND-ME-DOWN ETIQUETTE?

Throw out anything torn, chewed or stained. Only keep clothes in good condition for hand-me-downs. Pass on unwanted good items to charity, or sell on eBay.

✦

Newborn outfits are rarely used, as mothers receive so many as gifts and babies quickly grow out of them. Store as hand-me-downs for your next baby or pass them on to another mother.

✦

Remove any stains, and then wash, dry and store used baby clothes in plastic bags inside storage bins marked three months, six months, nine months, one year, etc. This makes life easier when your next child is born. Actually, nothing makes life easier when your next child is born. Except servants.

✦

It's a nice idea, for special clothes that have been handed down to you, to return them (if they are still in good condition) to the original owner with a small gift.

✦

Hand-me-downs always fit your child before you think they will.

✦

Before you give someone your child's hand-me-downs, ask if they want them. Some people take offence.

✦

Don't forget to share special-occasion maternity clothes with friends and family.

✦

It is okay to 'lend' items (including cots, high chairs, etc.) and request their return. You may want to keep a special outfit for future grandchildren.

ELEVEN SMART WAYS WITH CHILDREN'S CLOTHING

1. From the start, buy good quality mix-and-match clothing that does not need ironing, and embrace hand-me-downs from family and friends.
2. Dungarees look sweet, but are difficult for little girls as they have to get undressed to use the bathroom.
3. If your child is in day care, preschool or school, label all clothes and uniforms.
4. When you receive a gift of new clothing, photograph your child wearing it and send a photo with the thank-you note. This scores major brownie points with older relatives.
5. Deep drawers are no good for children's clothes. The things at the bottom will never be used.
6. Keep a change of your child's clothes (ones they rarely wear) and an old towel in the boot of the car.

7. If a visiting child spills something on their clothes, don't offer your own child's clothes until you have asked them if it is okay. There's a chance they will embarrass you by throwing a hissy fit.

8. Clothes hangers with crocheted or knitted covers are very useful – small clothes don't fall off them.

9. If you live near the beach or have a pool, keep all old swimwear. At some point, someone will need it.

10. Avoid dressing your different-aged children in identical clothes, as the smallest will end up wearing the same thing for many years.

11. Fashion-conscious children want labels – and there's nothing wrong in picking up a second-hand item from a charity store, cutting the label off and sewing it onto a cheaper item.

I'M NOT WEARING THAT!

One fine day when the sun is high in the sky and songbirds are rejoicing in the old oak tree, you'll pull an outfit from the wardrobe and a small voice will say, 'I am not wearing *that*!' What they mean is, 'I'm not wearing that ever again and if you make me I will ruin your day and the next fourteen years as well.'

Don't react.

You won't win this battle and you won't win the war. Troops at kindergarten have already fuelled the muskets and you have no ammunition. And that's because there really is no reason why your child shouldn't wear a fairy costume to the dentist, just as there's no reason they shouldn't walk across a sofa in socks, or drink melted ice-cream through a straw.

It's why women, not men, are mothers. No civilised society could have survived men's 20th-century rules – 'While you're under my roof' and all that nonsense.

Lord save us pretties – we'd still be wearing sensible cardigans over backless dresses until we turned thirty, and we'd never have boyfriends and never have children and the whole human breeding cycle would be stuffed good and proper.

SHOE TIPS

If your child is a monster shopper, draw around their foot while they are standing and take the drawing to the shop, instead of the child. Make sure you can return the shoes if they don't fit.

❖

Too-small socks can do as much damage as too-small shoes.

❖

Children will trip over if their shoes are too big.

❖

Shop for shoes in the late afternoon, as children's feet swell during the day.

❖

Velcro fastenings are easiest for littlies.

❖

Round shoelaces do not always stay tied – better to use flat ones.

❖

Buy shoes with soles that grip.

❖

Place a cut-down pool noodle inside leather boots to keep their shape.

TOP FIVE HAIR TIPS

1. Experimental hairdressing with scissors by the under-fives is quite common and not a sign you have produced an axe murderer. Don't panic. Visit a professional for style repair.
2. Ribbons easily fall out of hair. Tie a bow and sew it onto the ponytail band.
3. Use a detangling spray before gently combing wet hair, or mix ½ cup of conditioner and ½ cup of water in a spray bottle. Squirt on hair and massage in. Spray extra solution onto stubborn tangles.
4. A round, itchy bald spot with broken hairs near the scalp may be ringworm. If unsure, ask a hairdresser. If confirmed, or if you are still unsure, see your doctor for diagnosis and treatment.
5. Children who 'hate' water in their eyes can wear swimming goggles in the shower. It's difficult, but you can wash hair around the rubber strap.

HEAD LICE

Head lice are insects that can live on a human scalp. Hard to see, the lice lay eggs (nits), which 'glue' themselves to hair. The eggs are whitish and small and if found close to the scalp indicate a recent infestation. Head lice are not a reflection of poor hygiene and are common among children, so expect a few infestations during the early years.

SIGNS OF INFESTATION

Fine black powder (lice faeces) on the child's pillow.

✦

Lice can be seen moving among the hair.

✦

White specks (nits) are stuck to hair near the scalp.

✦

The child's scalp is itchy.

TREATMENT

There are many effective products on the market, most of which are a form of shampoo, and you should begin treatment immediately (you can use swimming goggles to keep the solution out of the child's eyes). If children share beds, or do not always stay in their own bed, it is a good idea to treat all family members at the same time. After treatment, remove eggs with a fine-tooth 'nit' comb, available from most pharmacies. This is fiddly, but it's the only way to remove the eggs. Repeat the treatment one week later to ensure newly hatched eggs are destroyed. Wash bed linen (despite advice to only wash pillowcases, it's usual to want to wash sheets as well, so just do it), combs and brushes in hot water and detergent.

TIPS

I used hairspray on my daughter's hair if there was an outbreak at school. It seemed to offer some protection.

✦

Always keep long hair tied back and make sure your child wears their own hat.

DEFY THE DRAMA OF GREEN POOL HAIR

Fair-haired children's hair may turn oddly green when repeatedly exposed to chlorinated water. Here are ways to mitigate the damage:

Wear a swimming cap (duh!).

✦

Wet hair under a shower before swimming – this offers some protection against chlorine damage.

✦

There are commercial hair products for swimmers that will remove a green tinge. Ask a hairdresser which is best, or check labels at the supermarket.

✦

Alternative method: Dissolve about six aspirin in a bowl of warm water. Rinse hair repeatedly with the solution, recycling by pouring over another bowl in the sink. You can also lay a child on a table with their head hanging off the end, hold the bowl and soak hair for as long as possible, then rinse normally.

HOW TO CUT A CHILD'S FRINGE

1. Hair must be dry.
2. Comb fringe forward and sticky-tape down across forehead.
3. Don't cut too short. Remember, hair will spring up 2-3 cm when tape is removed, so allow for this.
4. Taper fringe line down at outer edges so it doesn't look like you used sticky tape as a guide.

This method strikes fear in the hearts of suburban hairdressers, but I assure you it was the chop of choice when I was a student in London, and it did a roaring trade in our bathroom for many years.

HOW TO REMOVE CHEWING GUM FROM HAIR

Don't reach for the scissors and don't try to pull gum out while still gooey.

✦

Freeze with ice-cubes or an ice pack, and when it's rock hard, break and chip it off.

✦

On the internet, you will find various other chewing-gum-removal methods, including rubbing the gum with peanut butter, mayonnaise or warmed vinegar. They all seem to work.

BEST TIPS FOR A VISIT TO THE DOCTOR

Try to make the first appointment of the day.

✦

Take a list of symptoms and questions with you. It's easy to forget when you're sick, tired, or your child is unwell and screaming blue murder. For the same reason, write down the answers.

✦

Take your child's medications with you.

✦

If new medication is prescribed, ask about side effects and what to look for.

✦

Do not allow children to play in the specially provided play area of the waiting room. The toys are working germ laboratories.

✦

Don't be nervous about ringing the surgery if you have not understood what you were told. Many doctors are quite happy to call back or email you.

✦

Rather than removing a recipe from a magazine in the waiting area, take a photo of it with your phone.

FOUR BEST TIPS WHEN CARING
FOR A SICK CHILD

Always buy two bottles of analgesic/fever-reducing medicine for children. Then you won't run out at 2 a.m.

✦

Children pick up germs from toys in waiting rooms, super-market trolleys and play equipment in the park. Be mindful of this and wash their hands after they have been in contact with any of these things.

✦

Get to know your local pharmacist. They know a lot about illness and can offer information and treatment for many minor ailments. Many community pharmacies offer home delivery, which is great if you can't leave a sick child.

✦

Give children an ice cube to suck before administering unpalatable medicine. It numbs the tastebuds for just long enough. An ice cube can also be rubbed on skin before an injection or splinter removal.

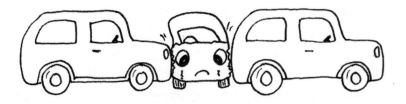

Every parking space in the world has a secret desire to humiliate mothers. The smaller the space, the greater the desire and the bigger the audience.

HERE'S A GOOD IDEA FOR HOSPITALS – SOMEONE PLEASE ORGANISE IT

Now that nurses no longer wear fancy uniforms and doctors are rarely seen in white coats, and everyone from the head surgeon to the hospital porter wears scrubs or similar attire, why don't they all wear paper caps advertising their positions? We need to know who you are, what you do, and if we should be telling you about problems in our lady gardens or other personal information.

GENERAL NURSING CARE OF A SICK CHILD

All children get sick, and quite often too. Most child-hood illnesses are mild and fleeting, but their frequency is astounding. So be warned.

Accept that you won't sleep for a day or two.

✦

Cancel social appointments – you'll be too tired to go.

✦

Do all the washing. Ignore other household chores.

✦

Prepare the sick room. Remove toys and things you might trip over in the dark and clear a surface beside the bed.

✦

Put the child's pillow in a large, well-perforated plastic bag and cover with a towel. This absorbs sweat and vomit and is easier to change quickly.

✦

Place a plastic protector and a bath towel across the bed under the child's body. They may have accidents when ill.

✦

Place tissues and a bowl on the bedside table in case of vomiting.

✦

Provide plenty of fluids but don't leave a jug and glass beside the bed because the child will knock it over.

✦

Place a plastic sheet (or a large bin liner) and a large bath towel on the floor beside the bed. Children like to throw up beside beds. Dogs too.

◆

Sick children are frightened children. Stay with them as much as possible, or at least let them be close enough to hear you if you're in another room.

◆

Keep the child clean and cool. Help with a shower or bath. They may revert to babyhood and need to be washed.

◆

Leave a light on at night, particularly in the bathroom. Sickness always seems worse in the dark.

◆

Open the windows if it's safe to do so. Sick children need fresh air.

◆

Change the child's clothing regularly. (This is why you keep up with the washing.)

◆

Offer small 'tastings' of food. Sick children do not need huge ham sandwiches. A little cracker with a thin sliver of cheese is more appealing. One strawberry and three grapes are easier than a vat of broth.

◆

Lemonade ice-blocks go down well, as they provide relief for sore throats and fevers.

◆

Give the child something to look forward to when they are better. No, not going back to school. Something nice.

◆

Very sick children don't need entertaining, but those with mild illness and those on the mend require a few distractions, such as movies and games. I'm afraid you will also be one of the distractions.

❖

Don't give the child a bell. They will drive you insane with it.

THE TEN ESSENTIAL MUST-DOS IF YOUR CHILD IS IN HOSPITAL

1. Be there as much as possible. If you can't be there as often as you'd like, fill absent times with other family members.
2. Try to appear calm and confident in front of your child.
3. Be honest at all times. Your child has to be able to trust you.
4. Take in a special familiar toy. Put your child's name on it.
5. Take in a security blanket if your child has one. Put your child's name on this, too.
6. If your child ignores or rejects you, don't be upset. This is not unusual.
7. Never sneak away. Always say goodbye if you have to leave, and perhaps give the child something of yours to look after until you return (sunglasses, hairbrush, etc.).
8. Try to fit in with the ward's routine. The nursing staff will advise ways you can help.
9. Remain with a distressed child even if your presence appears not to be helping. Only leave if staff tell you to.
10. Don't promise a going-home date in case this is postponed. Surprise is best.

WHAT TO TELL HOSPITAL NURSING STAFF

✦ your child's familiar name, i.e. Sammy instead of Samuel
✦ special words your child uses for the toilet, for drink, for being hungry, etc.
✦ allergies to food and/or medicine
✦ personal idiosyncrasies, such as fear of the dark or needing to sleep with a teddy bear or security blanket

WHEN YOUR CHILD COMES HOME
FROM HOSPITAL

The child's needs must now take priority over those of other family members for a couple of days. They will be unsettled for some time after a stint in hospital, and often tired. Expect:

✦ aggression/tantrums
✦ reversion to baby behaviour (bed-wetting, needing to be fed)
✦ nightmares
✦ rejection

Ignore it all and give love by the bucketload.

HOW TO SPOT A MALINGERER

Once, in a panic, I asked a patient to jump up and down because I had forgotten to shake his medicine. This same method can be used to spot a malingerer – if a child is well enough to jump up and down, then they're good enough for the Department of Education.

Mothers know real sickness instantly. There is something unmistakable about dull, sunken eyes and the resigned expression of defeat as a child surrenders to malady. Mothers also know that children can be fine one minute and very ill the next.

This creates something of a dilemma when we are presented with vague stories of a sore tummy and nausea, complicated by our prior knowledge of an imminent spelling test. You won't make the right decision every time, and when your phone rings and a stern voice informs you that your child told you they didn't feel well this morning and you must collect them from school at once, it's a real slap in the face.

ICKY BASEBALL CAPS?

Check the label for washing instructions and colourfastness and if it doesn't say 'hand wash', and it isn't an old or vintage cap, run it through a short gentle cycle in the top shelf of your dishwasher. This is less likely to damage the brim than a washing machine. If you don't have a cap form (available online) then position the cap carefully over prongs to maintain its shape. Use normal dishwasher detergent, but no bleach, and NO DISHES! Dry on a flat surface.

*If your child is afraid of a visit to the dentist, try
taking a little supporter along – often children will
be braver if they have a friend in tow.*

DIARRHOEA AND VOMITING (D AND V)

Children and babies will sometimes have a little diarrhoea
or an occasional vomit, and as long as it is a one-off and
doesn't continue, don't panic. However, if the diarrhoea or
vomiting (or both) persist, they may lead to dehydration and
then it's time to seek immediate medical help. Dehydration
is an ever-present danger with D and V, especially for babies
and small children. Make sure you know the signs.

SIGNS OF DEHYDRATION

+ urinary output reduces
+ continual vomiting
+ sunken eyes with dark shadows underneath
+ dry mouth, tongue and lips. No tears
+ skin is dry
+ child looks withdrawn and sleepy

**If your baby or child is showing signs of dehydration, seek
immediate medical help.**

Rehydration is also essential for children and adults with mild cases of D and V:

Purchase a commercial oral rehydration solution (only after checking that your child meets the age requirements for this).

✦

If you can't get to the pharmacy, use flat lemonade or flat cola, diluted with water. Give small amounts at frequent intervals.

✦

Do not give fruit juice to anyone with diarrhoea. It may worsen symptoms.

✦

Resume normal feeding slowly. Solids introduced too quickly can exacerbate the problem. Start with dry toast, crackers or boiled rice, not hamburgers and chips.

HOW THE BOWEL WORKS

If you have seen the marvellous poo machine (real name *Cloaca Professional* by artist Wim Delvoye) at Tasmania's MONA (Museum of Old and New Art) then you will have witnessed exactly what happens to the food that goes in one end and comes out the other – complete with authentic smell. (For those who haven't seen the poo machine, it consists of a series of chambers through which food and liquid pass, replicating the processes of the human digestive system in a sort of shunting moon walk.)

It's the same with the human body. By the time faeces arrive at the rectum most fluid has been reabsorbed, leaving enough moisture to make the stool soft and easy to pass; nature's way of ensuring that your bottom doesn't slam shut afterwards. Nerve endings recognise bulk in the rectum, signal for evacuation and bingo, it's out. Except sometimes it isn't.

WHAT IS CONSTIPATION?

Constipation is an inability to pass hardened faeces. It has nothing to do with regularity. Some people go every day like the 8.20 train from Central Station, while others only go twice a week. As long as faeces are softish and pass easily, there is no problem.

SIGNS OF CONSTIPATION IN CHILDREN

+ a distended tummy
+ frequent, quick trips to the toilet with no flushing
+ tummy aches
+ continual soiling of pants (the occasional skid mark can be put down to bad wiping but repeated stains can indicate leakage around a mass)
+ frequent small amounts of diarrhoea (this is leakage of new faeces entering the rectum and passing around the obstruction)

N.B. Bad breath is not a sign of constipation, but many adult males do become irritable if constipated (years of nursing taught me this).

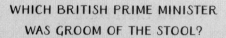

WHICH BRITISH PRIME MINISTER WAS GROOM OF THE STOOL?

The amazing role of 'Groom of the Stool' was created during Henry VIII's reign. Usually held by a nobleman, the holder of the position was the caretaker of the monarch's bowel motions. The groom ensured the monarch's diet was adequate, that mealtimes were regular, and that the commode, water and towels were available as required.

The position was well compensated both financially and with court favours. One such groom, John Stuart, 3rd Earl of Bute (???!!!), went on to become prime minister of Great Britain.

CONSTIPATION IN BABIES

You don't have to be Einstein to figure out when a baby is constipated – the lack of evidence is obvious. But regularity is not important. Look at the baby. If they are happy and well, and as long as the motion is abundant and soft, it's no problem whether they are going three times a day or once in three days.

Breastfed babies rarely get constipated, but those on bottles and solids occasionally do. If constipation doesn't resolve, and your baby looks unwell or distressed, seek advice from reputable organisations, your doctor or baby health clinic.

POSSIBLE CAUSES OF CONSTIPATION IN CHILDREN

Children sometimes ignore nerve-ending signals telling them to evacuate. Instead, they hang on and the faeces become harder and increase in volume, making evacuation painful and often impossible. They ignore the signals for several reasons, the most obvious being they are busy playing.

Other reasons can include:

It is not convenient to go (the signal often happens far from the nearest toilet).

✦

They are in a hurry and don't feel they have time.

✦

The school toilets are dirty and off-putting (this is a very common cause).

✦

A lack of privacy.

✦

They don't want to make a smell in someone else's house.

✦

They have hung on for so long they know it will hurt.

✦

They have a small tear or fissure from passing a previous monster.

The child may have a diet lacking in fibre and liquids. Nothing, but nothing, gets a mother's dander up more than someone criticising her parenting, so before you seek help and risk being told you are not feeding your child properly, ask yourself if maybe your cherub's body doesn't require more fibre and water than others, and give that a go.

THE MOST COMMON REMEDIES FOR CONSTIPATION

A diet containing plenty of fluids, fruit, vegetables, wholegrain cereals and bread. Bran for breakfast is a must for the constipated. Orange juice and a bowl of prunes are nature's dynamite.

◆

If your child is ignoring the call of nature, doesn't like school toilets or doesn't want to make a bad smell, try giving them private time (after breakfast) on the toilet.

◆

Gentle massaging of the tummy, especially after a warm bath, often does the trick.

If all of the above have failed, it's time to seek professional help. For one-off situations, the pharmacist can assist. Frequent constipation will require a visit to the doctor, who may prescribe a mild laxative. If the child has a small tear around the anus that has bled, don't fret. These heal quickly and the doctor may give you anaesthetic ointment to relieve pain in the meantime.

A word of caution: Some children's bowels react violently to immersion in cold water. This is why one occasionally sees Richard the Thirds floating in public swimming pools.

(Sensible mothers learn not to get wet themselves until they have dragged their offspring to the toilet. They also learn to sit near the public toilets at the beach.)

SEVEN THINGS A MOTHER NEEDS TO KNOW ABOUT LIVING WITH TEENAGERS

1. Teenagers get a bad rap and they don't deserve it. Most teens are gorgeous, funny, smart, sensitive individuals who are learning to be adults. Trust me, somewhere behind your brooding, obnoxious, uncommunicative screen junkie is a really cool human being.
2. You will be indispensable one minute, in the way the next.
3. You are the grown-up in the relationship and it is your job to love, guide and support your teenager as they ride the hormonal storm and find their place in the world. And it's not easy for either of you.
4. You don't need to win all the battles to win the war.
5. Teenagers say cruel, hurtful things to people who love them because they know it is safe to do so. Teenagers who are unsure of being loved by those that are supposed to love them don't say those things – they daren't.
6. You don't need to make a judgement call on everything they tell you. Sometimes it's good to just listen and thank them for telling you.
7. Teenagers believe they are the invincible chosen ones and it's all about them. You know they aren't and it isn't.

Shouting at teenagers used to be called
'Shouting at Teenagers'.
Today it is called 'Motivational Speaking'.

TEENAGERS WITH STRICT PARENTS TELL LIES. THEY LIE ABOUT:

✦ where they are going

✦ who they are going with

✦ what they are going to do there

✦ where they have been

✦ who they were with

✦ what they did there

✦ what they did at school

✦ what they didn't do at school

✦ which parents, if any, will be supervising at a sleepover or party

✦ why they are late home

That about covers it! Erring on safety, try to hit the middle road between rules and freedom.

❖ MEMO ❖

A survey of mothers waiting in cars outside a local high school
found that, fifteen years after giving birth to a child,
it is perfectly normal to experience moments when you
want to push them back in again.

SEVEN TEENAGERS WITH
SERIOUS STREET CRED

JULIET CAPULET: Juliet, lover of Romeo, was only thirteen years old in Shakespeare's play *Romeo and Juliet*. In her father Lord Capulet's own words, Juliet 'hath not seen the change of fourteen years'. Romeo's age is not known, but it's surprising that old man Capulet didn't murder him.

CATHERINE HOWARD: Although her exact date of birth is unknown, it is believed Catherine was about sixteen or seventeen when she married King Henry VIII in 1540 and became his fifth wife and Queen of England. She was eighteen or nineteen when Henry had her beheaded in 1542 after learning of her premarital affairs.

JOAN OF ARC: Born in France in 1412, Joan was a courageous peasant girl of eighteen who believed she was given divine guidance when she led the French army to victory against the English at Orléans. At nineteen she was captured by the English and burned at the stake for being a heretic. In 1920 she was canonised as Saint Joan of Arc.

TUTANKHAMEN: Tutankhamen was the most famous male pharaoh of all. He was only nine when he became King of Egypt around 1333 BCE and married his half-sister. He ruled throughout his teenage years until his death at nineteen. It was long believed he was murdered, but following scientific tests it is now believed he died of a broken leg (degenerative bone disease) and possibly malaria.

MARY SHELLEY: Born in 1797, British author Mary Shelley was sixteen and pregnant when she ran off to the Continent with the married poet Percy Bysshe Shelley. Two years later she married Percy after his wife committed suicide. At eighteen, Mary also started to write the best-known horror story of them all: *Frankenstein*. The book was published anonymously in 1818.

BOBBY FISCHER: Born in Chicago in 1943, Bobby Fischer was an American–Icelandic chess player who became the youngest chess grandmaster in history at fifteen. He left school at sixteen to devote his life to chess, and his eccentric personality and aggressive playing style brought the game out of the shadows and into the spotlight.

ANNE FRANK: Born in Germany in 1929, Anne Frank was a Jewish teenager who wrote a diary while hiding from the Nazis in a house in Amsterdam during the German occupation of the Netherlands in World War II. After being discovered by the Gestapo, Anne died in Bergen-Belsen concentration camp in 1945. Her diary was later published and has sold over 30 million copies.

HANDY HINTS FOR LIVING WITH TEENAGERS

You will have established rules and boundaries for using phones, computers and other electronic devices before your child reaches their teenage years, but be prepared for these rules and boundaries to shift sideways as your growing teenager's needs change.

✦

Remember that hormones are in charge, not you.

❖

Invest in a top-quality stain remover.

❖

Electronic drum kits with headphones are much quieter than acoustic kits.

❖

'It's in my room' is a euphemism for 'Get it yourself'.

❖

Try cultivating a 'Don't mess with me look' to counteract scoffs and eye rolls.

❖

Rory Soames does not get $50 a week pocket money.

❖

Ear piercing in the bathroom is not elective surgery.

❖

If your nineteen-year-old still hasn't left home, wrap their lunch in a roadmap of your nearest capital city.

❖

'I hate you, you're the worst mother in the world' is only valid until dinner or money for a movie, whichever comes first.

❖

Make sure sons know how to use the washing machine before they hit puberty – when they will suddenly want to wash their own sheets.

❖

Teens need tons of sleep. Let them snooze at the weekend.

❖

Family planning's finest hour is the unmerciful display of emotional combat between a menopausal chief-of-staff and a pubescent underling.

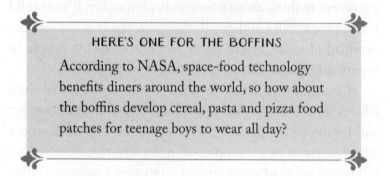

HERE'S ONE FOR THE BOFFINS

According to NASA, space-food technology benefits diners around the world, so how about the boffins develop cereal, pasta and pizza food patches for teenage boys to wear all day?

TEENAGERS' BEDROOMS ARE A HYGIENE HAZARD

It's their room. If they want to live in a pigsty, I say let them. Do not tidy – you may find something you don't want to know about – but if you suspect drug use, rip that room apart.

Keep the door closed to contain the smell.

Clean the room twice a year with industrial-grade chemicals.

Reclaim crockery once a month.

Let the dog in at regular intervals to scavenge pizza from under the bed.

THE BEGINNER'S GUIDE TO SHOPPING
WITH YOUNG CHILDREN

Ask yourself, 'Should I attempt this or not?' Then take a moment to think about your child's personality. If your child is compliant, calm and not bothered by the massive sensory overload of noise, bright lights and hordes of big people in supermarkets and shopping centres, then shop away.

If, on the other hand, you have a completely normal child who is split six ways till Christmas by noise, bright lights and hordes of big people, then you will have to make some adjustments to your shopping outings, like reminding yourself not to get mad when your child throws a wobbly, as they surely will.

EXPERT TIP

I came up with this tip in relation to shoes, but it also works with clothing. If you have bred a monster shopper and you need to buy clothes for them, lay the child on a large sheet of white butcher's paper and draw around them. Then cut out the shape and take the paper cut-out to the shops instead of the child. Just make sure you can exchange things if they aren't right.

THINGS I LEARNED FROM SUPERMARKET SHOPPING WITH A CHILD

I was given plenty of well-meaning advice about shopping with a child, like how to use the visit to a supermarket as a fun educational experience, and that it was good to let my child be involved with the shopping and choose some items and push the trolley. I was also told that it was a great way to teach my child about healthy food. I tried it all and here is my official report:

> Choosing four round, red, juicy apples was the easy part. Collecting up the 200 that tumbled off the display and rolled down aisle five was much harder.

> Old ladies and crouching shelf-stackers do not like being rammed by an out-of-control shopping trolley.

> The whole shopping experience was made so much worse when I had to spend another hour searching for a precious toy that it was suggested we take along to give my child something familiar to hold – a toy that had been discarded somewhere between the car park and the freezer section.

> It's really difficult to smile at impatient shoppers in the checkout queue as your child stands in the trolley and individually unloads everything at snail-pace onto the conveyor belt.

CONCLUSION: Shopping with young children was the blueprint for the Northern Ireland Peace Accord.

IF YOU MUST SHOP WITH A YOUNG CHILD, BE PREPARED!

Make a list of what you need and where you have to go.

✦

Don't shop on an empty stomach – this applies to both you and your child.

✦

Shop after your child has had a sleep.

✦

Don't shop at busy times – i.e. Saturday morning, after school or before dinner.

✦

Allow an hour more than you think you will need.

✦

Do the most important thing first.

✦

Carry bribes in your pocket.

✦

Take the child to the bathroom before you enter a supermarket.

✦

If you let your child push or hang onto the side of the shopping trolley there is a chance you will spend the next few hours at an emergency department.

✦

Do not even attempt the insane practice of meeting a friend for coffee. It won't work. You don't need to prove the child hasn't changed your life, because they have.

✦

It's time to embrace online supermarket shopping. It's easy, timesaving and the store will not give you poor quality produce as they want your repeat custom. You can either pick up the shopping or have it delivered to your door.

SASSY SUPERMARKET TIP

Hey, let's really use less plastic!

Instead of putting fruit and vegetables into the plastic bags they supply in produce sections at supermarkets (you know, the environmentally conscious capitalist organisations who now charge us for plastic bags), take a re-usable box (one you can wash), place it in the trolley and fill it with your purchases. You can unload the box at the checkout and refill it as the items are processed. Then the box goes into the car and afterwards into the kitchen.

Easy-peasy, and delicate fruit like peaches won't get squashed.

HELP!

If your child throws a gale-force tantrum in a supermarket, you can:

1. Move a short distance away, immerse yourself in reading a product label and pretend you aren't related to them. (I tried this and it doesn't work so well. The child pointing at me and screaming was a dead giveaway.)

2. Push the trolley of groceries to one side and take your child outside – to fresh air, if possible – give them a drink and if they have calmed down, then go back and retrieve the trolley. If they haven't, go home.

SIX KILLER REASONS WHY YOU SHOULD WIPE TROLLEY AND BASKET HANDLES AT THE SUPERMARKET AND THE AIRPORT

1. These handles are what scientists call 'fomites', which means they are objects likely to carry infection.
2. If you think this is over-the-top infection control, ask yourself this: why would you use disinfectant at home but then take no care with a piece of public equipment that might be harbouring a germfest?
3. It's possible the trolley or basket has been used by:
    a. someone with a nasty viral infection who has been coughing into their hands
    b. someone who has been to the bathroom and not washed their hands
    c. a parent who has sat a sick toddler (with an infection that would flatten your grandmother) in the trolley.
4. Many of us live in global communities where our neighbours are well travelled and the places we frequent are often visited by people from other parts of the world. It's therefore possible the trolley has been used by someone who has flown in from a cholera zone, or someone who has visited another hemisphere and picked up the latest influenza virus.

5. Picking up new germs to which you have no resistance does not toughen you up. It makes you sick, and can infect your family, friends and colleagues.

6. The same wiping-down advice goes for community keyboards and touch-screen check-ins and check-outs. They are all germ factories. You are not being overly zealous. You are simply being careful and trying to stay healthy.

FOUR

Back to the Paid Workforce

FOUR BACK-TO-WORK MINDFULNESS STRATEGIES

1. Acknowledge the new skills and fresh perspectives you are taking back to the workplace following maternity leave; the longer the leave, the stronger the skills.
2. Reflect on the positive aspects of returning to work – more money, adult conversation, getting dressed up and job satisfaction. This is important, particularly when so many jaded martyrs are launching rockets of terror from crucibles of negativity at you.
3. Accept that returning to work is challenging. Remember that millions of mothers do it and survive, and so do their families. So, if you have to return to work, it's best to scoff at any negative thoughts, pull on your big-girl pants and just get on with it.
4. Laugh at your new wobbly bits and be happy your old work clothes no longer fit. It can take ages for our bodies to return

to showroom condition, which means embracing the two most exciting words in the English language: NEW CLOTHES!

THIS MOTHER WINS THE PRIZE FOR MOST UNUSUAL COMMUTE

In November 1984, American chemist, emergency-room doctor and NASA astronaut Anna Lee Fisher became the first mother in space when she flew as a mission specialist on the Space Shuttle *Discovery* STS-51A. To prepare and train for the flight, Anna had returned to work at NASA a few days after giving birth in 1983. In a NASA video, she said, 'I was assigned to my flight two weeks before I delivered my oldest daughter. I remember I delivered Kristin on a Friday and I was at the Monday morning eight o'clock meeting the following Monday.' Fourteen months later, Anna was the first mother in space.

Remember: there is no such thing
as a non-working mother.

THE UNBELIEVABLE MARRIAGE BAR

For much of the 20th century, legislation called the marriage bar restricted married women in parts of the English-speaking world from professional paid employment, including education, nursing, teaching and the public (civil) service. It also dismissed women from their existing paid professional roles if they got married.

Unfortunately there are still about eighteen countries where wives need their husband's permission to work, and over a hundred countries with laws preventing women from having certain jobs. For example, women can't drive trains in Russia, work underwater in Bangladesh or drive tractors that run at over 50 horsepower in Vietnam – all of my favourite things, so I won't be going to live in any of those places.

UPDATE YOUR RESUME

When a mother returns to the workforce after being at home with babies and children, she has hands-on experience in the following areas:

- time management
- organisation and planning
- multitasking
- working well under pressure
- problem-solving
- decision-making
- patience
- communication
- conflict resolution
- perseverance
- tolerance
- sleep deprivation

N.B. You might leave that last one off your list, although it's true.

SEVEN THINGS WORKING MOTHERS DO EVERY DAY

1. Think evil thoughts about celebrity chefs who have raised everyone's dinner expectations.
2. Say 'Oh shit!' when they remember something they've forgotten to do.
3. Wonder what their children are doing.
4. Use the bathroom mirror to check if the stain on their shirt is visible.
5. Wonder if anyone would notice if they climbed under the desk or into a cupboard for a snooze.
6. Completely ignore a phone call.
7. Consider leaving a jacket on the back of their office chair at work and slinking off early.

WISE WORDS

When you return to the paid workforce after maternity leave, don't feel as though you have to prove yourself.

You have not forgotten all that you knew on the day you left work, and while you were away you made another human being in your body – it's a little hard to top that!

A SMALL BUT IMPORTANT QUIZ

Q1. When was the last time you heard a mother asked how she juggles work and motherhood?

Q2. When was the last time you heard a father asked how he juggles work and fatherhood?

My answers are probably the same as yours: Q1. Not long ago. Q2. Never.

The important takeaway here, and I apologise for generalising but it does partly explain the discrepancy, is that subconsciously we all know that most working mothers still do the lion's share of housework. Therefore working mothers do three jobs – paid employment, motherhood and housework.

Fathers, for the most part, only do two jobs, paid employment and fatherhood, which might explain why they are never asked how they juggle things.

SUBJECT FOR DISCUSSION AT
THE WATER COOLER

What if governments allowed working mothers a tax deduction for employing someone to clean their house while they are at work?

Would there be happier, healthier and more productive working mothers?

Would there be happier and healthier marriages and partnerships?

HANDS UP IF YOU UNDERSTAND WORK–LIFE BALANCE?

Work–life balance is a perplexing term on so many fronts. It assumes that all work is paid work. It ignores volunteering. It ignores housework. It implies that one part of the work–life equation is not as good as the other and needs balancing out. It suggests work is not something positive that we might enjoy or be proud of, and infers that we might need to do less of it.

The reality is that everything we do in our waking hours is part of our life. Awake–asleep balance would make more sense to working mothers as there are times when the crown weighs heavy on our heads.

THE BEE'S LAW: BE WARNED. BE CAREFUL

Returning to work part-time can be a great option, but success greatly depends on the type of work you do. Practical workers – for example, pilots, nurses, paramedics and those in the retail or hospitality industries – fare well as productivity is achieved within the allocated hours and little, if any, work is taken home.

Other occupations are not so kind. The boss expects 40 hours' worth of work from a 24-hour-a-week schedule and before you know it you're taking work home, feeding a baby propped up by cushions, working on a laptop and texting on a phone, and Anglo-Saxon words are coming out of your mouth and steam is coming out of your ears.

So be warned. Part-time work can have a real sting in its tail.

THIS HAS GOT TO STOP

Working mothers have got to stop feeling guilty for working. It's insane, but many mothers feel they are being judged as selfish women for abandoning their children for some personal gain.

Ridding mothers of this guilt is a tough task, as judgement is constantly coming at us from all sides – the media, research institutes, university studies and ill-informed members of the public.

In an effort to assuage this guilt, many mothers put themselves at the bottom of their priority list, ignoring their own needs and spending too much time and money compensating their families for this nonsensical perceived selfishness.

SO STOP IT!

> **REMINDER**
> *Mothers who are not in the paid workforce do not have to travel to work. They just get up and it's all right there in front of them.*

DID YOU KNOW

Behind every successful woman is a man looking at her bottom.

TWELVE UGLY TRUTHS THAT EXPLAIN WHY MOTHERS RETURN TO PAID WORK

As part of my conversations with different mothers on the ferry to Taronga Zoo (captive audience from across the globe), I asked them if they had returned to work after having children and why they did so. Their answers showed that mothers return to the workforce after having children either because they want to or because they have to. And within those two reasons are other reasons.

Here are the main responses:

I love my job, it's part of my identity and I want to maintain a career path.

✦

I have to contribute to the family income to cover our mortgage, household bills, etc.

✦

My partner is unemployed or unable to work, so I have to.

✦

I'm part of a business and integral to its success.

✦

I'm a single mother trying to provide for my family.

✦

I can work from home.

✦

I couldn't stand being at home all the time.

✦

I need/want financial independence from my partner.

✦

I have teenagers and I was going mad at home.

✦

I want a secure financial future and a decent superannuation
for my retirement.

✦

I have more job security/satisfaction and/or higher remuner-
ation than my partner.

✦

I work in the family business (or on our rural property) but
don't get paid.

CONCLUSION: We are all different mothers in different
situations trying to do the best we can. Or in the memorable
words of Brenda from Newcastle, England, who was visiting
her son in Sydney, Australia, 'I had to work, pet. I married a
right lazy sod, me. Thought he was too special to work. Honest,
pet, if he'd been made of chocolate he'd have ate himself.'

OUR CHILDREN LIVE IN THE REAL WORLD

Recently I was brought to boiling point by an article
proclaiming that working mothers, no matter how hard
their day has been, should consistently greet their children
at the end of the day with enthusiasm and good humour.
I am guessing the writer was talking about robots, so let me
be the first to poop on that inhuman proclamation with my
own little gem:

Consistency is for psychologists, sauces and wet cement.

WHAT DO MOTHERS DO ALL DAY?

Superwoman is alive and well and living at my house and yours. She is running a home, bringing up children, texting family and friends, booking dental appointments, making birthday cakes, exercising, volunteering at school, mowing lawns, hanging out washing, fetching groceries, watching kids' sports, cooking meals, painting ceilings, burying mice, paying bills, helping with homework projects, entertaining friends, making costumes, wrapping gifts, walking dogs, and many go to work as well. And that's just Monday. No one knows what she does the rest of the week. Oh, more of the same, is it?

SIX SMART THINGS TO DO BEFORE MATERNITY LEAVE

1. Establish your entitlements and responsibilities with your employer.
2. Establish your rights, responsibilities and entitlements under the law.
3. Advise HR of your anticipated leaving date as soon as you can, to allow time to source a maternity leave replacement.
4. Establish your anticipated date of return and try to make it midweek so that Monday is over and the weekend is closer.
5. Ask if you can build up your work days over several weeks. Some mothers shorten their overall maternity leave by a week or two and use those days to shorten their first few weeks back at work.
6. Ask if you can have flexibility of work hours when you return to work – and obtain the response in writing.

SIX SMART THINGS TO DO WHILE ON MATERNITY LEAVE

1. Establish a circle of friends who are also mothers with young babies. You will need their friendship and support as your children grow, especially when you return to work. Nurturing these friendships is incredibly important. It's paramount.
2. Keep up networks and communication with work colleagues and stay up-to-date on your workplace/industry news.
3. Make a date to take your baby/child into work before you start back. And take a cake. It's good for co-workers to meet your offspring and good for small children to know where you will be.
4. If you will be expressing milk when you return to work, give your boss or HR advance warning so that time and privacy will be accommodated. Ascertain which fridge you can use.
5. Practise your work face in the mirror as there will be times during the first few days back when you will feel overwhelmed and will zone out. You are going for a cross between interested and thoughtful with a hint of surprise. This also scares off slackers trying to palm their work off onto you.
6. There's no reason why we can't have fun. Organise new work clothes. Your body has changed and may take time to return to its original size and shape, if ever. Obviously you will sort out clothing closer to your return date.
   - If you are breastfeeding you will need larger tops (I expect you worked that out). Dark tops are better at hiding leakage, and they're more flattering, too.
   - If you wear a uniform at work, organise the required size.

- Visit an op shop for second-hand designer basics – skirts, pants, jackets, etc. Buy new shirts that don't need ironing.
- Alternatively, seize the day and reinvent yourself with a whole new style – bohemian, 1950s, gypsy, preppy, elegant, vintage, chic, sophisticated, whatever.

NEVER APOLOGISE FOR BEING A MOTHER

Almost without exception, mainly because it is our bodies that make babies, it is the mother who compromises her career and daily work patterns to accommodate family needs. That is why mothers in the workplace should never apologise or justify the reasons for having to do something because they are a mother. Never refer to your time off work to have children as being 'unemployed' on your resume. Never apologise for having to leave a meeting to express milk. Never apologise for having to leave work on time because you have a child to collect. 'I have to go now and I have my phone if you need me' will suffice.

Working mothers serve two types of meals – take it or leave it.

CAUTION

Even though you are overflowing with maternal love and you want to share pictures of your gorgeous offspring with colleagues, please don't email photos to work of your baby covered in whatever they are eating. Just don't do it, okay?

A QUESTION OF EQUALITY

Who decided that what men have and are is what all women want and need? Certainly we should have equal pay, equal access to education, jobs, positions, promotion, health care, financial security and a host of other things, but mothers are different human beings to men. Whether we adopt or make other human beings in our bodies and feed those human beings from our bodies, our responsibilities to ourselves and others are different to those of men. Our wants and needs are different as well.

We must never be complacent or forget that it wasn't so long ago that women had no control over their reproductive system and couldn't work if they were married. And we must always remember that others fought hard for our rights, and it is our duty to keep the flame alight. We must never take our eyes off the ball.

PLANNING YOUR RETURN TO WORK:
THE BIG FOUR

1. **BUDGET**: Similar to starting a new business, prepare a family budget that includes anticipated incomings and outgoings. Outgoings should include extra transport costs, childcare, cleaner, new work clothes, etc.

2. **CAREER GOALS**: Apart from extra income, think about what you want from your job or career – the skills you want to learn, the promotion you are aiming for, or projects you want to undertake. Where do you want your career to be in a year? In five years? Do you want to be doing the same job? Might you try something else? It's good to have something to work towards, apart from a month alone on a desert island without a phone.

3. **CHILDCARE**: Research your options, establish what you need and what is available to meet those needs, and then organise childcare well before you return to work. You also need to organise a back-up person for emergencies. Almost everything you need to know about childcare, including advice for grandparents providing childcare, can be found online on government-funded parenting websites.

    a. Look for childcare that is provided in a clean, safe environment with professional staff. If you are not confident about the care, it will be difficult to successfully return to work.

    b. Make a list of questions you want answered and visit a few childcare centres. There is nothing wrong with waiting outside and asking emerging parents for their opinions of the centre and care provided.

c. Remember: No childcare worker will love your child. In fact, the more someone talks of their love for your child, the faster you should probably make for the door.

d. A word of caution: Babies and children who attend childcare can get sick quite often. Despite the rules, some working parents will deposit a dosed-up, unwell two-year-old at childcare, and before you know it there are twenty-five sick children, one of whom is yours. As many grandparents now share childcare duties by looking after their grandchild one or two days a week, if the child also attends a childcare centre on other days, the grandparents may get sick quite often too. And they won't be happy about that.

4. **HOUSEWORK**: If you have a partner, then they should agree to do 50 per cent of the housework when you return to work. If they don't agree, then the cost of hiring someone to clean the house once a week while you are at work MUST be factored into the budget. This will save your sanity and possibly your relationship. Have the cleaner start a couple of weeks before you return to work so you get to know each other and they learn how you and your partner like things done.

THREE SURPRISES THAT AWAIT YOU AT WORK

1. The sheer joy of going to the toilet alone.
2. You will feel guilty for feeling happy.
3. You will have two logical thought processes in a row. Celebrate this, but don't share it, and aim for three.

TEN THINGS WORKING MOTHERS WANT

1. A personal assistant (we can dream).
2. For ill-informed people to stop firing guilt-laden bullets at working mothers.
3. Flexible hours and flexible days – that include, perhaps, working from home, working on Sunday, working school hours, or incorporating hours into a four-day week.
4. Childcare in the workplace.
5. An established group of supportive mothers who can help each other when needed – when running late for pick-up from school or childcare, etc.
6. Job-share opportunities.
7. Paid maternity leave.
8. To say NO without feeling guilty – and for teachers, relatives and friends to understand that working mothers have to say NO often.
9. If our jobs can support it, to be able to work from home when our children are sick.
10. Childcare that doesn't cost more than we are being paid.

A woman's work is never dumb.

IF YOU ARE WORRIED THAT YOU MIGHT HAVE GONE A LITTLE NUTS WHILE ON MATERNITY LEAVE, TAKE THIS SIMPLE TEST TO SEE IF YOU ARE READY FOR THE WORKPLACE:

Have you seen Elvis this week?
If so, was he in a UFO?
There you are. Absolutely nothing to worry about.

SHORTLY BEFORE YOU RETURN TO WORK

Make sure you are competent with the breast pump and milk storage.

✦

Start your baby/child in childcare before you return to work so you are not establishing new routines for both childcare and work at the same time. In the beginning, spend time with your child before you leave and gradually reduce the time you stay to a few minutes.

✦

Prepare a list for the childcare provider of your family-specific baby words (i.e. 'bot-bot' for bottle) that you use at home.

✦

Attend to your image. Do what you can afford – a good easy-care haircut and tinted eyelashes are top of the list. This will help you feel more like a professional than a milkmaid on day release.

✦

Buy a clipboard and attach some paper to it. This will be your prop at work if you need to cover milk leaks on the front of your shirt. It is also something to pick up as you leave your desk for privacy when tears start to flow, and is excellent if you need to walk around looking like you are doing something when you are really regrouping your brain cells while moving.

✦

Plan meals for the first week. Have frozen dinners at hand in case of emergencies. This is no time for gourmet cookery or trying interesting things with quinoa.

✦

Plan your outfits for the first week. You won't have the brain space to make simple decisions like what to wear. In fact, cut down on as many decision-making tasks as you can.

✦

Prepare a plan to work from home in case you have to.

✦

Decide what you will do about social media with colleagues. Remember, what's on there, stays on there. Apart from the usual avoidance of profanity, rumours, dirty jokes, threats and personal details, don't post any information about work-related matters (a competing company might like to know you are two weeks behind on a submission), pictures of your children tagged with their names, complaints about your boss, organisation or workmates, and things your colleagues should be sharing themselves. From personal experience I can tell you that it's not a good idea to refer to Human Resources as Human Remains, that it's really stupid to refer to your boss as half man half nose (even if it's true), and definitely not a smart move to boast that it was you who put the Twister mat in the lift.

✤ MEMO ✤

Working mothers have a right to reinvent themselves as often as they want.
Examples:
From tomorrow I will put night cream on my neck before going to bed.

✦

From tomorrow I will smile all the time and talk softly like Deborah Kerr in The King and I.

✦

From now on I will start exercising for thirty minutes every day.

✦

I will never go to work with wet hair again (apropos this, dry shampoo is great if you don't have time for the full experience).

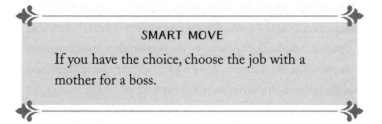

SMART MOVE

If you have the choice, choose the job with a mother for a boss.

FIRST WEEK BACK AT WORK

Take a large box of tissues. You will be weepy, but this will pass. (It's also why you should have an eyelash tint.)

✦

It is perfectly normal to want to hide.

✦

You will quickly realise you have a new perspective on what matters most in the world.

✦

Take your entitled breaks.

✦

It is okay to call your childcare provider to see how your child is. In fact they expect it, and might think it strange if you don't call.

✦

Celebrate that you can use the bathroom without having to call out 'What?!'

✦

Do not talk about nappies and sick, and roll your eyes if anyone else mentions them. Parenting is about so much more.

✦

Breastfeeding? Keep clean shirts at work in case of leaks, which will happen.

✦

Put your name down for any short courses on offer during work hours. Sometimes this involves sitting still and looking like you are listening. You will be very good at this.

✦

A good work productivity tip is to write DO NO DISTURB on a Post-it note and stick it on the side of your face. I do this a lot. Once, I wore one to Woolworths.

✦

If you buy dinner supplies during your lunch break, put your car keys in the bag you put in the fridge. That way, you won't forget the bag. Well, that's the theory. If you don't drive to work, stick a Post-it note on your handbag.

✦

If you feel the need to curry favour, brown-nose or reinforce your commitment to work, ask a senior employee for their report from the last conference they attended.

✦

Do not resign when the day arrives that you are overwhelmed by work and home and lack of sleep and you have a melt-down. It happens to all mothers, and if it doesn't happen to you then you are not trying hard enough. Pick yourself up and dust yourself off. Tomorrow is another day, kid.

◆

Be kind to yourself. Things will get easier. And harder. And easier. And then one day you will think, 'Hot damn, I can do all this.'

AND YOU CAN!

MY SECRET SHARED

If you are not shopping online for groceries to be delivered, and you enjoy choosing your own food: SUPERMARKETS ARE THE LEAST CROWDED ON WEDNESDAYS.

Mothers never retire. But don't worry. We live longer because we get to sit down every time we go to the bathroom.

WORKING MOTHER'S MANTRA: STAY CALM AND CARRY ON

Apart from new protocols, new staff and 40,000 emails awaiting you upon your return to work, the first month back will be an emotional rollercoaster as you grapple with the highs of being back in the grown-up world and the lows of sadness about being separated from your baby. But you won't have time for any poor-me-boo-hoo stuff because:

Family members will take it in turns to get sick, usually with something that requires round-the-clock nursing and disinfectant by the bucketload. And they will give the bug to you.

✦

There will be a problem with the public transport you catch to and from work.

✦

Every person under ten will lose the ability to feed and dress themselves.

✦

The baby will sense tension, become fractious and won't eat or sleep.

✦

There will be many media reports of maternal neglect caused by working mothers.

✦

The car transmission will break.

✦

The hot-water system will break.

✦

Your glasses will become lost or break.

✦

The dog will need to go to the vet.

✦

Someone will come to stay for a few days.

✦

The goldfish and/or the guinea pig will die.

✦

Someone will eat the packed lunches you prepared the night before.

✦

Homework will be due but not done.

❖

The dishwasher will flood.

❖

One child will bring a lamb home to be looked after to help farmers during the drought.

❖

The dog will wee on the carpet and start eating furniture while you're out.

❖

All children will lose their bus passes.

❖

If you make it to work you'll be phoned to collect a sick child from childcare or school.

On the upside, this will all settle down, and the next time a work colleague complains that one of the team is breathing too loudly and disturbing everyone you will smile and start to sing 'The Wheels on the Bus' and see how they cope with that. Often, other mothers and fathers will join in.

IT'S NOT ALL ABOUT THE CHILDREN: WHY MORE RESEARCH IS NEEDED

There's plenty of data available to help parents make informed decisions about their children's futures. However, most research involving working mothers, regardless of the research title or suggested aim, is focused on the positive or negative effects a working mother has on a child's development and wellbeing. It's not about the mother at all – although one time, when I was researching astronauts, I did find out that menstruation is not affected by space travel. Good to know. Thank you. I'm sharing the info.

It's not widely acknowledged, but most mothers are smarter than your average Border Collie, and we already know the results of research studies way before the research study starts. As in, we already know that the results will tell us exactly what the organisation that funded the research want us to hear. Nice try, but we're on to you.

We don't need research to tell us that working mothers are time-poor multitasking queens – we already know all that – but data on the conflicting emotions a mother experiences when she has to surrender a six-week-old baby to childcare in order to return to work is conspicuous in its scarcity.

I want to see more research on the good and bad long-term benefits on our mental health of returning to work, when is the best time for us to return to work, how many hours should we do, and what are the long-term physical effects and stress on our minds and bodies of returning to the workforce while continuing to lactate and breastfeed another human being.

In other words, we would like more research on our own development and wellbeing so we can make informed decisions about our own future. I'll get off the soapbox now.

FIVE

Order in the House

Mothers no longer apologise for the mess when a visitor arrives.
We do not recognise the ancient homemaker paradigm that a
tidy home equates with our value as a woman and mother.

I drew this sketch of Quarry Farm, Mark Twain's summer home, on a hot summer afternoon while sitting in his garden high up on Watercure Hill Road in Elmira, New York.

Twain wrote major portions of his most famous works in an octagonal study in the garden that has since been moved to Elmira College in town.

After a while, a pleasant-looking man walked up to me and told me the property was not open to the public, but instead of throwing me out we chatted about Twain and it became apparent to him that I was a Twain fanatic. Smiling, he told me that he was there to prepare the house for a visiting Twain scholar who was arriving that day from Germany, and he would let me have a quick look-see in the house. I think my heart stopped for a few seconds, only recommencing with the shock of hearing myself offer to help him clean the house. He politely refused and we entered. Breathing in deeply of the air, I walked on floors where Twain had walked, touched walls and doors that Twain had touched, and closing my eyes I sat in the room where Mark Twain and Rudyard Kipling, arguably two of the greatest writers of all time, had talked back in 1889. The experience remains one of the most precious moments of my life. And it also remains the only time I have ever wanted to clean a house.

HEALTH WARNING!

HOUSEWORK CAN KILL YOU

Housework is dangerous. Stroll down the aisle of cleaning products in any supermarket and you'll find a poison or other health warning on almost every item.

SO GO VINEGAR AND BICARBONATE OF SODA, AND SAVE YOURSELF AND THE PLANET!

FIVE MORE THINGS MOTHERS WANT

4. Four pillowcases in every double, queen and king sheet set – not two.
5. Self-cleaning windows.
6. Plastic lids that clip over the base of shaving-foam cans to stop rust marks on bathroom surfaces.
7. Ride-on vaccum cleaners.
8. A prominent label on the short side of all fitted sheets.

'AN ENGLISHMAN'S HOME IS HIS CASTLE'

Long before women could own property, this 17th-century phrase from English politician and lawyer Sir Edward Coke referred to the legal precept that no one (and that includes the Queen) may enter a person's home unless by invitation.

This precept was established as common law in England in *The Institutes of the Lawes of England* in 1628. It's occasionally cited in court as a defence for violence against an intruder in a home, but it absolutely does not give anyone the right to bash someone senseless in their home, or take any other action inside their home that would be illegal outside.

FIRST GOLDEN RULE OF THE HOUSE
Play with your child more often than you clean your house.

HOUSEWORK, CIRCA 1915

'It is considered perfectly acceptable in these times, once the house is clean and tidy and the washing and ironing put away, for the housewife to take a short nap and lie on the kitchen floor.'

I found this comment in the housework section of an old American book of the *Enquire Within upon Everything* genre.

I expect the man who wrote it is dead. I certainly hope so.

FOUR FAMOUS MEN WHO ONCE WORKED AS JANITORS

American rock star Jon Bon Jovi worked as a janitor at a New York recording studio.

Canadian comedian Jim Carrey worked as a factory janitor for two years after leaving school.

American musician and singer Kurt Cobain worked as a janitor at Weatherwax High School, Washington.

American author Stephen King also once worked as a high school janitor before writing the bestselling novel *Carrie*.

REVEALED: THE FIRST STEPS TOWARDS ORGANISING YOUR HOME

PAPERWORK
Pin onto a corkboard anything for which you need a visual reminder – ads, upcoming events, tickets, to do lists, etc. Purchase a plastic filing box with runners for file inserts and file all household paperwork. Set up folders on your computer for bills, receipts, etc., that arrive by email.

WARDROBE
Arrange hanging clothes by colour – all blacks together, all greens together, etc. This instantly makes getting dressed easier.

UNSIGHTLY ELECTRICAL CABLES
Go online or to a hardware store and buy cable covers or something similar to hide your spaghetti tangle of exposed wires.

ELECTRONICS CENTRE
Source a chest of drawers to act as a tech centre and place it near a power outlet. All electronic gizmos will be charged on top. Ensure one drawer is deep enough to hold DVDs and/or CDs on their side so labels can be read (stacked DVDs gather dust). All electronic connections, computer and printer parts, instruction booklets, spare cables, batteries, Kindles, spare phones, portable hard drives, etc. go in the drawers.

PANTRY

Buy three large plastic containers with different coloured lids that fit on your shelves. Place baking needs (flour, sugar, baking powder, nuts, shredded coconut, etc.) in one, different types of rice in the second and pasta in the third. Don't bother with labels – you'll get used to what's in each box by the colour of the lid.

CUSHIONS

You are not living in the window display of a bedding store. Get rid of the piles of cushions on your bed that serve no functional purpose and are in the way. However, a fabric strip across the foot of the bed is a good idea if you lie on your bed in your shoes (yes, unlike the cushions, this fabric has a purpose).

BITS AND PIECES

Establish a 'junk' drawer in the kitchen. Use it for safety pins, spare keys, coins, badges, nuts and other odds and ends you don't know what to do with but may need later.

TOYS

Buy large storage boxes or cubes for children's rooms and hurl everything in (the toys, not the children).

SCHOOLBAGS

These monsters gravitate to the side of the fridge because that is the first port of call by the owner seeking food, but be firm about this: schoolbags go straight to the owner's room.

IRONING

The fastest breeding pile in the house, ironing is a depressing sight and should never be visible. Put it out of sight. And if you can afford it, find someone to do your ironing.

WHY MOTHERS NEED A ROOM OF THEIR OWN

As mothers tend to run the family home, it stands to reason that mothers might need a nerve-centre from which to operate things – such as a room of their own.

If you are lucky enough to have a spare bedroom, hit the internet to sell the big bed and replace it with a sofa bed, then turn the room into an office, studio, study, or person-in-charge type of room. You'll never need to tidy the room or put things away (unless guests are coming), and because the mess is yours, you won't be bothered by it. If you don't have a spare room, set up a table in or near the kitchen and put a sign saying 'MINE' above it.

Also, think seriously about abandoning the formal sitting/living room (or whatever you call it) if you have one – it's nothing but a subversive method to perpetuate the ridiculous notion that a house requires a special room in which to entertain guests. And it doesn't give you a place to relax away from the children because:

You might not want to be away from the children.

❖

The things you need to relax with are never in the formal room.

❖

The furniture in the formal room is uncomfortable and marks easily.

✦

All guests congregate in the kitchen anyway.

Common sense should tell you that if there is a spare room or space, it should belong to the mother. I think Virginia Woolf would have agreed with me.

THE BIGGEST PROBLEM WITH CLEANING (AND THE SOLUTION)

You start to clean one thing and are distracted by cleaning something else – and on it goes until you've moved all the furniture, everything is half-done and the place looks like it's been vandalised.

The only thing that will focus you on cleaning what's needed quickly is to invite someone over. That will make you blitz the place in thirty minutes.

WHERE WOULD YOU FIND A FLYING TOILET?

A flying toilet is the name given to a plastic bag that someone has defecated into, tied with a knot and thrown out of their front door. You would find flying toilets in the streets of Kibera, a large slum in Nairobi, Kenya, as Kibera is located outside the planned sewerage system in this capital city.

THREE TERRIFIC TIDYING TRICKS

1. Pick a tabletop in a central spot to act as a repository for everything. Put all stray items on it – basketballs, library books, homework, sweaters and things to be fixed. This confines many small messes to one large mess, which you will learn to overlook.

2. Play a game. Move around the house and put away ten things in every room. Anything in the wrong room goes on the repository table. Sometimes I change things up by aiming to put away one hundred things in the whole house, but I cheat and count the cutlery as I unpack it from the dishwasher.

3. Play a different game, this time with other players. (This only works with children under ten – everyone else makes rude gestures at you from behind walls.) Instruct the players to stand by the repository table then order, 'Jack, put the home readers in your schoolbag and report back to me. Frankie, put the hat in the cupboard and report back to me.' N.B. You have to think one chore ahead to avoid players wandering off.

OH, THAT DIRTY WORD

The label 'housewife' has singlehandedly created the misconception that cleaning a house (housework) is a wife's domain.

I think we should all remove it from our hard-copy dictionaries with a black marker. Librarians, this is your call to arms!

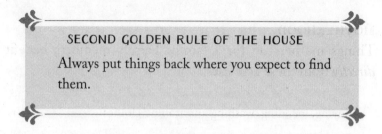

SECOND GOLDEN RULE OF THE HOUSE
Always put things back where you expect to find them.

MOTHERHOOD VS HOUSEWORK:
A SCIENTIFIC BREAKDOWN

FACT ONE: Motherhood is a different job to housework.
FACT TWO: Motherhood is caring for people. It provides rich emotional rewards.
FACT THREE: Housework is caring for a house. There is no emotional reward – just the blind fury you feel when all your hard work is wrecked within half an hour.

Consider the following:

HOUSEWORK
Things many mothers do for a house. Family members benefit *indirectly* from these activities:

Dusting, polishing and sweeping.

✦

Cleaning bathrooms, scrubbing toilets and washing floors.

✦

Vacuuming carpets, cleaning windows and polishing mirrors.

✦

Cleaning the kitchen, cleaning the oven and defrosting the fridge.

MOTHERHOOD

Things mothers do for a family. Family members benefit *directly* from these activities:

Buying, mending, washing and ironing clothes.

✦

Planning meals, shopping for food and cooking.

✦

Getting up at 2.30 a.m. to tend to the sick.

✦

Creating and sewing concert and event costumes.

✦

Helping with homework.

✦

Washing sheets and changing bed linen.

✦

Acting as a taxi service.

✦

Et cetera, et cetera, et cetera.

The difference is profound, isn't it? Housework and motherhood are two separate jobs. Anyone can do housework. Motherhood, on the other hand, requires skill, patience and a variety of talents that are quite simply impossible to quantify. (It's worth noting that many fathers tend to opt for family chores that provide emotional rewards, preferring to grocery shop and cook rather than clean toilets and vacuum.)

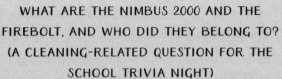

WHAT ARE THE NIMBUS 2000 AND THE FIREBOLT, AND WHO DID THEY BELONG TO? (A CLEANING-RELATED QUESTION FOR THE SCHOOL TRIVIA NIGHT)

They are both broomsticks owned by Harry Potter. The Nimbus 2000 was Harry's first broom. The Firebolt was a racing broom given to Harry for Christmas by Sirius Black.

RUN OUT OF DISHWASHER DETERGENT? MAKE YOUR OWN!

Put three drops of dishwashing liquid into the usual detergent receptacle. Fill it two-thirds with baking soda (bicarbonate of soda). Add salt until almost full. Close cover and run dishwasher as normal.

N.B. There are several homemade dishwasher detergent recipes online.

CLEANING YOUR DISHWASHER

Pour 1 cup (250 ml) of white vinegar into the bottom of an empty dishwasher and run on the normal cycle. Do not put vinegar in the detergent dispenser or beneath the dishwasher trap.

DISHWASHER TIPS

If you use dishwasher tablets, try putting a tablet in the bottom of the dishwasher (not under the trap) instead of in the dispenser. This seems to work better with some dishwashers.

◆

Use your dishwasher regularly or it will smell. Leave the door ajar if you're going away.

◆

The top tray on most dishwashers can be lowered for tall glasses or raised for large plates in the bottom tray.

◆

Try using half the dishwashing powder you are presently using.

◆

Scrape food scraps off dishes before packing. Pips and pine nuts can block the drain pump and non-return valve.

◆

Run the hot tap in the kitchen sink until hot water comes through. Then switch on the dishwasher. It will fill with hot water and take less time to heat up.

◆

Unpack the bottom tray first. If you empty the top first and you're called away, when you return, someone's coffee dregs will be dripping on the clean plates in the bottom.

◆

Stack cutlery with spoons in one slot, forks in the next, etc. This makes for easy unloading.

◆

Check your insurance policy. If the dishwasher leaks, your household policy may exclude floor coverings. On some policies, floor coverings are covered on contents insurance.

✦

Do not wash Lego in a dishwasher. The bricks may change shape in high heat and won't work anymore. Instead, clean Lego with warm water, mild detergent and a sponge, and rinse thoroughly.

THE WORLD'S FIRST SOLAR HEATING SYSTEM FOR A HOUSE WAS INVENTED BY A WOMAN

Born in Budapest in 1900, Maria Telkes was a Hungarian–American biophysicist and research engineer who invented the world's first solar heating system, and was recognised as one of the world's foremost pioneers in the use of solar energy. Known as the 'Sun Queen', Telkes also invented the world's first solar oven.

In 1948 Telkes worked with architect Eleanor Raymond to build and install her heating system in the Dover Sun House in Dover, Massachusetts, USA During World War II, at the request of the American government, Telkes also invented a successful solar water-distilling system for making seawater potable (safe to drink).

Telkes died in Hungary in 1995, aged ninety-four.

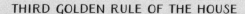

THIRD GOLDEN RULE OF THE HOUSE

Don't put anything in the middle of the most frequently used table. You will be forever moving it.

THE THREE MOST EXPENSIVE HOUSES IN THE WORLD

1. Owned by the Crown and home to Queen Elizabeth II, Buckingham Palace in London is the world's most expensive house. There are seventy-eight bathrooms to clean and I worked out that it would take me almost two weeks to wee in all of them.

2. The world's second-most-expensive house, and the most expensive privately owned one, is 'Antilia' in India. Owned by India's richest man, Mukesh Ambani, the 27-storey house can be found on the prestigious Altamount Road, Mumbai.

3. Owned by Brazilian philanthropist and mother Lily Safra, the historic Villa Leopolda on the French Riviera is the world's third most expensive house. This beautiful villa was used as a filming location for the 1955 Hitchcock classic *To Catch a Thief*.

LOST SOMETHING?

All missing crockery is under someone's bed.

THE WORLD'S ENVIRONMENTAL HEALTH

The Environmental Performance Index (EPI) is a joint project between Yale University and Columbia University, produced in collaboration with the World Economic Forum. The EPI provides a quantitative basis for comparing and analysing the environmental performance of 180 countries and their standing on a core set of environmental issues. Here is a snapshot of some of the 2018 rankings:

1: Switzerland

2. France

6: United Kingdom

13: Germany

17: New Zealand

21: Australia

25: Canada

27: USA

52: Russia

120: China

142: South Africa

177: India

180: Burundi

DISORDER IN THE HOUSE

ADULTS

Grown-ups are highly creative in mess design and location, and although things are improving, many seem genetically predisposed to create small repetitive messes such as wet towels left on beds, beard shavings on soap, axle grease in sinks and empty leftover plates in the fridge. I'm not sure which adults do this but if I think real hard it will come to me.

CHILDREN'S ROOMS

Whoa! The only thing to do here is to confine the mess to its own box or pile. Children's rooms need a good clear-out once a year, but keep detritus for two weeks in case of, 'Mum, have you seen a little pink dinosaur made of paper?'

LITTLIES

Very young children like to play where you are. By the day's end, the house is a toy shop. Tell them to take everything to their room and then do it yourself while they wander off. This is not how you would like it to be, nor how we are told it should be – but it is how it is. Don't lose sight of the desired result – toys away, calm mother and happy child. Never say you will throw away their toys if they don't tidy up. This is wicked and mothers are never wicked.

TIDY MARY

Tidy Mary is the name of the helpful person who, while you are busy frying onions, tips the stock that you have just made down the sink and washes up the jug.

A MAJOR OBSTACLE

This is usually an adult in the house who has never tidied up and has no intention of tidying up, but they will start barking around the house about children tidying their rooms. Off with their heads, I say.

INEFFICIENCY

There is a tendency by those who have waved the last child off to school to stretch the housework/tidying lark to fill the whole day. You will be excused for two months. This is the time it takes to absorb the deliciousness of having twenty-five hours each week when you can complete a sentence, an email, a phone call or a task without interruption. After that, you need to pep up the time-management skills.

FASCINATING AND COMPLETELY TRUE

In the remote outback opal-mining town of Coober Pedy in South Australia, where the desert winters are freezing cold and the summers are sizzling hot, people live in houses that are built underground. Called 'dugouts', the houses are amazingly stylish and comfortable and maintain a liveable temperature throughout the year of extremes.

Many other buildings in Coober Pedy are also underground, such as churches, restaurants and hotels. There is also an above-ground golf course without a single blade of grass.

MY MOST POPULAR HOUSEWORK HACKS

Clean the front door. First impressions and all that jazz.

✦

Put small ornaments that need dusting in a box marked 'For Retirement'.

✦

Dust wearing a sock on your hand – someone else's, of course. Then throw the sock in the washing machine.

✦

Stay away from houseplants. They are dust traps and always in some stage of disease or death – at least they are at my place.

✦

Have windows cleaned professionally twice a year. Any real estate agent will tell you that if the windows are clean the whole house looks sparkling.

✦

Shining sinks also give the impression of a total makeover. Each morning I wipe ours out with someone else's towel and then hang it up for them (I'm very thoughtful).

✦

Never vacuum alone. There is no point in zooming around the floor plan without annoying anyone but yourself. Let them see what a ghastly job it is. Suck up their papers, sabotage their phone calls.

✦

Never do today what you can put off until tomorrow.

HOW TO CLEAN A MICROWAVE

1. Pour the juice of one lemon into a microwavable bowl.
2. Place the bowl on the turntable and microwave for three minutes.
3. Leave for five minutes. Remove the bowl and wipe the inside of the microwave.

A DELICIOUS IRONY

Isn't it wonderful how many cleaning products are named after men?

MR MUSCLE
MR SHEEN
MR CLEAN
MR SHINY PANTS
DUSTER DICK
(I made those last two up.)

FOR DISCUSSION: THE GREAT WASHING MACHINE AND DRYER DEBATE

In the United Kingdom, many washing machines are in kitchens, which is a good idea if you lack space elsewhere. Because it rains twice a week in the UK (once for four days and once for three), many households use a dryer or dry their clothes near the boiler, but whenever they can, the British love to harness wind and solar power by hanging washing outside.

In Australia, many washing machines are in a dedicated laundry that has a rarely-used dryer, and as Aussies also love to hang washing outside, many backyards boast a rotary clothes line called a Hills Hoist – an Australian icon that starred in the opening ceremony of the 2000 Sydney Olympics.

In America, many washing machines are located in the basement of homes. I think this is because Americans like to carry large bundles of laundry up and down stairs. As a nation they appear to be terrified of line-drying, even having community and homeowner association laws forbidding the activity in many areas.

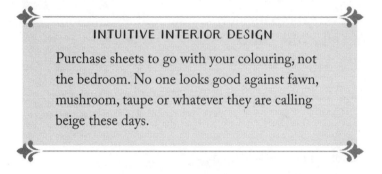

INTUITIVE INTERIOR DESIGN

Purchase sheets to go with your colouring, not the bedroom. No one looks good against fawn, mushroom, taupe or whatever they are calling beige these days.

WASHING POWDER

A word of caution – some soap powders are strong. Residue left in clothes and bedding may irritate skin and can cause rashes on babies, children and adults, particularly at sweat points and in the knicker department.

Next time someone in the family has an unexplained rash, your washing powder might be the culprit.

WASHING AHOY!

When I was a child and my family lived in the South Downs of England, drying the washing at our house was a ceremonial performance.

My father, Herbie J., was a master mariner and had somehow acquired two ships' masts, which he planted at either end of the back garden to support a washing line. The line was attached to lanyards at both ends and raised on a pulley system, like hoisting a sail. You pegged out at half-mast and then heaved it all upwards.

Our laundry was a landmark for local aircraft, flying as it did way above the house. You could also see our washing from my classroom at Wykeham House in Fareham High Street. I never lived that down.

THE MAD, MAD WORLD OF REAL ARTISTS WHO LOVED TO PAINT REAL WOMEN DOING LAUNDRY!

- *The Laundress* (1886) by Henri de Toulouse-Lautrec
- *The Laundress* (1877–79) by Pierre-Auguste Renoir
- *Women Ironing* (c. 1884–86) by Edgar Degas
- *Washerwomen* (1888) by Paul Gauguin
- *A Woman Ironing* (1873) by Edgar Degas
- *The Washerwomen* (1780) by Francisco Goya
- *Woman Ironing* (1904) by Pablo Picasso

I wonder how many of these women would have been great artists if they'd had the luxury of time?

FAMOUS FICTIONAL HOUSEKEEPERS
(NASTY AND NICE)

✦ Mrs Danvers is the malevolent head housekeeper at Manderley in the novel *Rebecca* (1938) by Daphne du Maurier.

✦ Mrs Fairfax is the kind and loyal housekeeper at Thornfield Hall in the novel *Jane Eyre* (1847) by Charlotte Bronte.

✦ Mrs Hudson is both loyal landlady and long-suffering housekeeper to Sherlock Holmes at 221B Baker Street, London, in the Sherlock Holmes novels (published from 1887 to 1915) by Sir Arthur Conan Doyle.

✦ Esther Summerson is the sweet, kind orphan who becomes housekeeper at Bleak House in the novel *Bleak House* (1853) by Charles Dickens. Another loyal housekeeper in the same novel is Mrs Rouncewell at Chesney Wold.

THE NOT-SURPRISING ORIGIN OF
'SPRING CLEANING'

The term 'spring cleaning' heralds from bygone days when homes were closed up during winter to keep the cold weather out. Inside, the houses were lit by candles and gas lamps, and heated by open fires using coal or wood, so everything got dirty and smelly from the fumes and soot.

As soon as warm, dry weather arrived in spring the doors and windows were thrown open; furniture, furnishings and rugs were dragged outside and everything, including the inside walls and floors, was thoroughly cleaned to remove the winter grime.

THE FIX-IT BOX

This makes a thoughtful present for a new homeowner. Buy an attractive box and fill it with an assortment of the items listed below.

- araldite
- two types of screwdrivers
- superglue
- pliers
- scissors
- electrical tape
- stapler
- safety pins
- sticky tape
- dressmaker pins
- black laundry marker
- sewing needle/thread
- Blu Tack
- wooden skewers
- white-out
- two types of light bulbs
- elastic bands
- drawing pins
- bulldog clips
- tape measure
- paperclips
- ruler
- pens/pencils
- compass
- nail clippers
- ball of kitchen string
- rubber/eraser
- pack of AA batteries
- puncture repair kit
- picture hangers
- paintbrush
- hammer
- plastic lids for glue-mixing
- fuses

- ❖ tube of Polyfilla
- ❖ penknife
- ❖ torch with batteries
- ❖ tap washers
- ❖ sheets of sandpaper
- ❖ adhesive labels

- ❖ extension cord
- ❖ tweezers
- ❖ tin of plastic wood
- ❖ bandaids
- ❖ assortment of nails/screws
- ❖ set of hex (or allen) keys

PLOP, PLOP, PLOP

If you have a dripping tap that won't be fixed for days, tie a piece of string around the faucet and trail the end into the sink. Water will then run down the string rather than drive you mad with constant dripping.

DRINKING GLASSES, BOWLS OR OTHER CROCKERY STUCK TOGETHER?

Stand stuck items in hot water and pour cold water into the top vessel. After a minute or two, gently ease things apart.

WHAT'S IN A DOOR-KNOCKER?

Quite a lot if you live in the beautiful city of Kashan in Iran where many old homes have retained the tradition of having two door knockers – a round fat one and a long thin one. The sound of the knockers differs, alerting the home owner to whether there is a man (the long knocker) or a woman (the round knocker) at the door.

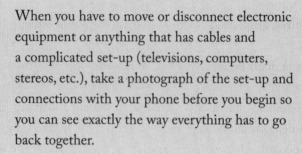

HOT TIP

When you have to move or disconnect electronic equipment or anything that has cables and a complicated set-up (televisions, computers, stereos, etc.), take a photograph of the set-up and connections with your phone before you begin so you can see exactly the way everything has to go back together.

HOME SAFETY

Lower the hot water temperature on your thermostat.

Never leave a baby or small child alone in a bath.

Run cold water through the tap after running a bath to prevent the child being scalded by the hot faucet.

Place a rubber mat in the bathtub to prevent slippage.

Remove electrical equipment (hairdryers, etc.) from bathrooms.

Discard unused medications and place the rest in a locked cupboard.

Don't leave other children to supervise a baby in the bath.

Place razors and other sharp objects out of children's reach.

✦

Knives, glasses and sharps should also be out of reach.

✦

Oven doors become very hot, so beware.

✦

Household chemicals (kitchen, bathroom, laundry and garden) should be kept out of reach of children in a locked cupboard. Dishwashing powder is caustic and extremely dangerous so put that out of reach as well.

✦

Immobilise cupboards with childproof locks.

✦

Use the rear hot plates and keep saucepan handles pointing towards the back of the stove.

✦

Secure the kettle or jug so leads don't drape over benches. Fit a cup hook behind the kettle and thread the lead through it for safety.

✦

Don't leave cups of coffee or tea on low surfaces.

✦

Stairs should be fitted with a safety gate.

✦

Check batteries in smoke alarms and replace if necessary.

✦

Lower door handles so children can escape in a fire (door handles in some older homes in Australia are located closer to the top of the door.)

✦

Safety-plug all unused electrical sockets.

✦

Remove all precious breakables from common areas.

✦

Cover sharp corners with padding or plastic covers (available from hardware stores).

✦

Don't put baby bouncers on tables. They can rock off the edge.

✦

Use caution if microwaving baby's bottles. The milk heats quicker than you think.

✦

Secure bookcases by bolting the top to the wall.

✦

Blu Tack a cork to each end of the piano lid to avoid slammed fingers.

✦

Live in an apartment? Secure children's windows so they cannot fall out.

✦

Gardening equipment (shears, secateurs, etc.) should be stored well out of reach.

✦

Place a fireguard around ALL fires. Never leave a child alone in a room with a fire, even if it is guarded.

✦

Keep lighters and matches on the top shelf of a kitchen cupboard.

✦

Do not leave a baby unattended in a pram outside in the garden unless you have a safety net cover to protect them from being smothered by a cat.

✦

Reduce the length of chords on blinds. Children can get them wrapped around their necks.

THREE USES FOR WD-40 THAT YOU NEVER THOUGHT OF

(Always use in a well-ventilated area.)

1. A quick burst of WD-40 will help remove a stuck ring from a swollen finger.
2. If you have superglue on your skin, give it a squirt with WD-40, then rub the area and the glue will come off.
3. Easily remove doggy-do from the soles of shoes with a quick spray of WD-40 followed by a scrub with an old nailbrush. Then rinse off.

A NOVEL WAY TO CLEAN A TOILET

1. Drop one or two denture tablets into the toilet bowl. The water will turn blue and start to work on stains.
2. Using a toilet brush, scrub at stains. You may need to use elbow grease for stubborn stains.
3. Leave for about 30 minutes, then flush.

MOVING HOUSE

I live with someone who knows a thousand ways to move to another house without using a furniture removal company. Trust me, I've carried a few sofas in my time. Fortunately, our last move covered an enormous distance, so we had to use the real thing – two strapping chaps and a big truck.

CURIOUS THINGS TO CONSIDER

Young children sometimes think you are going to move the actual house and worry things will be forgotten – like neighbours. Others are hoping you are moving to a tree house. If children haven't seen the new place, show them photographs, and decide which room they will sleep in. Make a game of it, give them a box and let them pack some of their things. Later, check the box for food and pets.

◆

Never assume that old bit of wood in the garage is just an old bit of wood in the garage. Someone will have been saving it since 2010 for a specific project. Pack it.

◆

Don't start renovating the minute you move into a new house. Wait until you know what works and what doesn't, in particular why certain trees and shrubs are where they are. That big bush could be hiding next door's washing line. That big tree might be shading the verandah in high summer. So pack away the chainsaw for now.

◆

If you move teenagers away from their friends, they will not speak to you for weeks. There's an upside to everything.

THE TOP THREE SECRETS OF
FREQUENT MOVERS

1. Leave clothes on hangers and (from the bottom) pull a large plastic bin bag up over the clothes. Secure it at the top with string around the neck of hangers so they don't fall into the bag. Label clearly and move clothes using your own vehicle.
2. Using one bin bag for each drawer, put contents into the bags. Then it's easy to unpack at the other end. Alternatively, stack drawers and contents on the back seat of your car to transfer.
3. Put sheets, pillows and blankets that you will be using immediately in a large plastic bag to transfer in your vehicle so beds can be made up in the new place straight away.

TOP MOVING TIPS

Something always goes wrong with organising utilities (power, phone, internet, etc.), so it's best to expect it. Then you won't be disappointed.

✦

Don't get super thingy about children being traumatised by a move. Take a deep breath and remember that many people in the world don't have a roof over their heads. Ever.

✦

If you can, move on an early weekday when children are at school.

✦

Use sturdy packing boxes, available from removalists and some hardware stores. Use good-quality masking tape.

✦

Use smaller boxes for heavier items (books, etc.)

✦

Prominently label all boxes with what room they are to go in at the other end.

✦

Use butcher's paper to wrap fragile items. Then you won't have to wash off newspaper print.

✦

Pay someone to clean the old house after you have gone. You don't want cleaning to be the final memory of your last home.

✦

If you can, organise somewhere for pets to stay for a few days.

✦

Make children's beds as soon as you arrive at the new place, and with familiar bedding that they like.

✦

Plan to eat at a nearby restaurant the first night and make a reservation.

✦

If self-moving, take the opportunity to break that dinner set you've always hated.

✦

Wrap kitchen liquids, like olive oil and vinegars, in cling film before packing.

✦

Read fine-print in the removal contract (will they put beds back together, etc.)

FIVE GOOD REASONS A MOTHER DOESN'T NEED A HOLIDAY WEEKENDER

1. You will be doing the same things you do at home, only in a different place without the proper equipment.
2. There are now two places to look after.
3. You are either packing or unpacking.
4. Ingredients you need are always in the other kitchen.
5. On return to home base, the kids settle down wonderfully relaxed after a two-day sojourn while you prepare dinner, iron school uniforms and commence round one of the laundry . . .

NO THANK YOU.

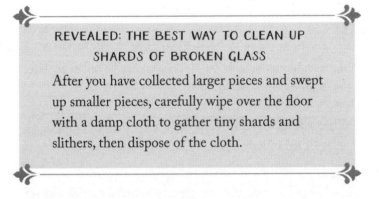

REVEALED: THE BEST WAY TO CLEAN UP SHARDS OF BROKEN GLASS

After you have collected larger pieces and swept up smaller pieces, carefully wipe over the floor with a damp cloth to gather tiny shards and slithers, then dispose of the cloth.

GIVE OUR HOMES BACK A REAL KITCHEN!

Someone has stolen the heartbeat from our kitchens. Picture this: a warm and friendly kitchen with everything for the cook to hand, a window overlooking the garden, a big table centre stage where a servant is kneading dough (I always have staff in my daydreams), oodles of chairs, a crackling fire, plates warming over the oven, bottles and spices on shelves, saucepans hanging from the ceiling, and a dog asleep in the corner.

It was a perfect sanctuary but someone had to wreck it. Kitchen police felled walls and chromed the cook into the corner of a vast void known as the 'family room', where the TV rules and furious frowns are directed at blenders and sizzling onions.

I'd like to know why the kitchen tap is often the focal point of many modern homes, standing high and arched over a sink. And why are kitchens being turned into stainless-steel monstrosities? You don't see celebrity chefs cooking in autopsy rooms.

THREE TOP USES FOR BABY POWDER

1. It's a good shoe deodoriser. Sprinkle into sports shoes and sneakers after each wear.
2. If the outside cover of your laptop has become sticky, you can return it to smoothness by sprinkling with a little baby powder and rubbing it in with a dry cloth.
3. It works as a carpet deodoriser. Test a small patch first and if all is good, sprinkle over a larger area, leave for ten minutes, then vacuum up.

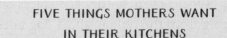

FIVE THINGS MOTHERS WANT IN THEIR KITCHENS

1. A fridge with a white-wine dispenser.
2. Large print on quantity measurements (e.g. ¼ cup or ½ cup) on recipes.
3. Convenient sachets containing 2 tablespoons of flour.
4. A self-cleaning oven.
5. Someone else cooking dinner.

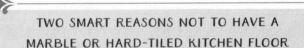

TWO SMART REASONS NOT TO HAVE A MARBLE OR HARD-TILED KITCHEN FLOOR

1. Your back will start to ache if you spend too long standing on a hard floor.
2. Everything you drop will break – including yourself, if you trip over.

Go for flooring with 'give', like cork tiles or wood.

THREE GREAT TIPS FROM THE SAVOY HOTEL, LONDON

When I was younger, as a protest against the pathetic wage I received as a state registered nurse, I resigned from King's College Hospital in London and worked for a month as a chambermaid at the famous Savoy Hotel – for roughly the same pay.

Here are my three great Savoy housekeeping tips:

Climb into a bath to clean it – we had to at the Savoy because the baths were so large, but I still do it (in bare feet).

✦

Place a large fold at the base of the top sheet before you tuck it in – this gives tall people more space for their feet.

✦

Place a boiling kettle under a hanging item of clothing to steam out the creases (the actor Raquel Welch taught me this when she was dressing for a premiere).

THREE SMART REASONS NOT TO HAVE GLASS DOORS ON KITCHEN CUPBOARDS

1. Unless you own antique china, you don't need to see your hodgepodge of old mugs, plates and cups from five different sets.
2. The glass can easily break.
3. It's an ongoing battle to keep frequently used glass doors clean.

Glass cupboard doors in kitchens are best left to homes photographed in magazines.

Position Vacant

THIS JOB HAS YOUR NAME WRITTEN ALL OVER IT!

I wrote the original text for this advertisement twenty years ago. After initial publication in Australia the ad appeared in international publications, was translated and printed in obscure foreign journals, and over the next few years it tripped the light fantastic across the globe via *Reader's Digest*, the internet and emails.

Since then, the world has changed. Technology has advanced, partners are more involved in home duties and parenting, and more mothers are in the paid workforce, hence major tweaks were required. So here it is, digitally remastered, unplugged, in real-time, and any other marketing speak that is used to make something old appear new again . . .

<u>WANTED:</u>   MOTHER!

<u>REMUNERATION:</u>   Nil

<u>ESSENTIAL CRITERIA:</u> Female

DESIRABLE CRITERIA:

1. Flexible, well-paid employment outside the home with opportunities for the incumbent to pursue family responsibilities throughout the workday.
2. A relative who owns a pub.

POSITION DESCRIPTION:

A multitasking self-starter, the applicant will be part of an exciting and dynamic team of go-getters in a competitive domestic environment. The applicant will be doing the going and getting.

POSITION REQUIREMENTS:

MARKETING

As the face of the team, and in keeping with current commercial images of designer motherhood, the successful applicant will maintain the mask of professional success, personal fulfilment, emotional control and confident sexuality when in the public domain. It is a standard requirement of the position that the incumbent is able to smile while gritting their teeth during parent–teacher interviews. Professional development will be provided for this.

MANAGEMENT

Applicant will hold a master's degree or equivalent in business administration and be directly responsible for damage control of failed budget estimates. Expertise in long-range planning is fundamental to the position, as is the ability to present personal opinion as proven fact during heated discussions with junior team members. Integral to the anticipated core management skill set will be the ability to field complaints and negotiate resolution in a manner that reflects our team esprit de corps. Applicants with experience in achieving bloodless outcomes to skirmishes over access to video games will be well-suited to the position.

COMMUNICATION

Maintenance of all communication networks between management and non-management is required. The applicant will be responsible for fielding enquiries 24/7, documenting off-hand verbal messages, and participating in video and teleconferences while a junior team member is hanging off their left leg and banging a saucepan with a soup ladle. The successful applicant will be required to provide sustenance to teenagers during lengthy periods on social media to avoid the medical effects of prolonged stasis, and will facilitate inter-personal family connections by relaying information between team members who are not speaking to each other.

IT CONSULTANT

Proficiency across all forms of electronic media and infor-mation technology is essential. A specialised knowledge of robotics may be required. Applicant will have expertise in extracting unwanted sandwiches that have been inserted by children into CD and DVD equipment owned by senior relatives. Applicant is expected to receive other team members' outdated phones and computers as birthday gifts and show appreciation for same. Applicant will pay for other team members' new devices.

CHAUFFEUR

Applicant will have the capacity to control a packed vehicle in heavy traffic while listening to a choking baby, a barking dog and factional infighting between passengers. Applicant will be adept at dodging wayward missiles emanating from a punch-up on the back seat, skilled at negotiating roundabouts while fielding questions on mating tortoises as seen on National Geographic, and competent at refuelling a vehicle while explaining that mooning passing cars is not socially acceptable. Applicant will know the location of every public toilet on the eastern seaboard.

CHEF

Applicant will be proficient at planning and preparing meals for all age groups, appetites, special diets and team members who will not eat anything green. Supply of own milk to new offspring will be regarded as a bonus, as will the ability to successfully disguise essential dietary requirements for the under-fives. It is expected the position will cater for cake stalls, school fetes and charity drives at short notice, assist in the operation of a canteen for 400, and prepare packed lunches for students who won't eat them.

NURSE

A seasoned stayer, the applicant will be immune to infectious diseases, capable of going without sleep for six days while completing other duties, and have the intestinal fortitude to clean up bodily fluids at two in the morning. Applicant should be on first-name terms with the GP receptionist and hospital emergency-room staff, be able to provide reassurance that ambulance sirens do not signify an alien invasion, and be capable of holding down someone they love while a stranger jabs them with a sharp needle. Expertise in stain removal is highly sought after in this category, as is knowledge of splinter removal, bandaging and acne medication.

ENVIRONMENTAL ENGINEER

Awareness of geothermal energy, polar ice caps and the exact location of Nemo are prerequisites for the position. Applicant must be able to demonstrate exceptional verbal restraint when responding to accusations by junior team members that senior management are murdering rainforests. Collection of unwanted food and refuse from behind furniture and under beds will be ongoing, as will stewardship of the worm farm after the owner has lost interest. Separation of recycling and haulage of household waste to the street is required. This will all be done at 5 a.m. because the person whose job it was forgot.

EARLY CHILDHOOD EDUCATOR

Applicant will have university-level education in botany and zoology, possess in-depth knowledge of all characters created by A. A. Milne, J. K. Rowling and J. R. R. Tolkien, and be cognisant of everything ever written anywhere about dinosaurs. The successful applicant will be responsible for explaining to junior team members why swiping a finger across paper pages in library books is ineffective, why their father's pedometer should not be attached to next door's Yorkshire Terrier, and why Pokémon is not a blood sport played with sharp objects from the kitchen drawer. The ability to make necklaces from macaroni and dental floss will be well regarded.

TEACHER

Applicant must be capable of working to deadlines. Essential to the position are the capacity to understand 'education-speak' in the form of directives from the school office, and an ability to decipher incomprehensible and ambiguous home-work questions. First-year university-level mathematics is an advantage, as is knowledge of Japanese, the complete works of William Shakespeare, the geographical structure of the Nile Delta, and the construction of the Niagara Falls hydro-electric generating stations. The applicant is expected to complete school projects at 5 a.m. on the morning they are due.

TAILOR

Applicant will have the talent to produce at short notice a costume for Book Week, the creativity to turn old curtains into Star Wars outfits, and the expertise to design and sew twenty-two rabbit costumes for the end-of-year concert. Other requirements will be maintenance of soft toys, repair of school uniforms, attachment of six million sequins to ballet costumes, and completion of discarded class cross-stitching projects intended for Mother's Day. Proficiency in construction of fairy wings using wire coat hangers, old panty hose and glitter is essential.

HAIRDRESSER

Applicant will be required to detect and treat head lice, remove chewing gum from hair and cut a straight fringe while receiving verbal and physical abuse. Reparation of severe damage to hair due to scissor experimentation by the under-fives will be required. Skills in paint removal will be an asset, especially following use of a junior team member's new buzz cut as a paintbrush. Restoration of socially acceptable hair colours will be necessary for teenagers who don't read packet instructions.

BIKE ENGINEER

It is anticipated the applicant will be conversant with all aspects of bicycle maintenance, including fitting and removal of training wheels. Applicant must be able to recognise their offspring at a distance of 200 metres, transform an ordinary bicycle into an armoured tank, repair punctures at a camping site 45 kilometres from the nearest garage, and convert Great-Grandma's old wheelchair into a go-cart. A first-aid certificate is required.

VETERINARY ASSISTANT

The position is expected to care for and train a variety of pets after the original owner has relinquished their position. Frequent feeding and cage-cleaning of malodorous rodents will be required, as will occasional care of a sheep from the school agricultural plot. Applicant must excel in time-scheduling to allow for animal exercise, and be well-versed in neighbourhood dispute resolution. Occasional burial services will need to be conducted.

COUNSELLOR

Applicant must be a good listener and hold a Certificate IV in conflict resolution. Mediation between outside forces and family members will be required, and an ability to resolve complex playground relationship issues using judicious bribery is an advantage. The applicant will be able to effect-ively placate senior relatives when junior team members remove the browser shortcut from their desktop, and will have the aptitude to successfully negotiate peace between two gladiatorial four-year-olds fighting to the death over a yellow dump truck. Resolution of intergenerational fisticuffs at mealtimes will be your forte. Counselling sessions will often be held while you are in the bathroom. Applicant is expected to complete doctorate in psychiatry as preparation for the teenage years.

GARDENER

Applicant must be proficient at starting a temperamental lawn mower, working with blunt gardening equipment and keeping houseplants alive. In the event of consumption of non-edible greenery by a junior team member, the position is expected to liaise with the national poisons centre. It is also anticipated you will be abreast of the latest methods regarding blotting-paper bean cultivation and repair of unintended tree surgery. Applicant will excel at arranging flowers with no stems in a vase, and know the location of all dogs, cats, mice and goldfish buried in the garden over the last twenty years.

PERSONAL TRAINER
Applicant will be responsible for laundry, leadership and team-building, and will coordinate sporting activities via electronic media and frequent trips to the school office. Participation in sports day events is required, as is presentation of chocolate bars to all losers on the way home. The applicant is required to attend home and away games in all weathers and encouraged to enter into strong verbal discussions with opposing teams. Purchase and maintenance of expensive equipment is expected, and presentation at fracture clinics will be ongoing. Pre-dawn attendance at swimming venues and ice rinks may be required.

ENTERTAINMENT OFFICER
An artistic all-rounder, the applicant will have the creativity to transform a dining table and sheets of corrugated cardboard into the Sagrada Familia, be across all important calendar dates, and have the patience and imagination to facilitate themed parties for junior team members having an emotional meltdown. Baking of cakes resembling cricket bats, ballet shoes and Barbie will be necessary during the early years. Applicant is expected to progress to complex presentation cakes depicting a gossamer-winged fairy princess riding a silver-spangled unicorn, the launch of a Saturn rocket during a thunderstorm, and a saltwater crocodile eating a Great White shark. The position will involve producing

jellies covering the entire colour spectrum and inventing games where everyone wins.

And the incumbent will do Christmas.

N.B. Candidates who excel in baking sugarless treats and cakes made from vegetables will not be considered.

SEVEN

Wanderings

A TRUE ROAD TRIP STORY

Some years ago my family took a road trip through New South Wales. My husband and I were sharing the driving, and our daughter, aged four, was calling the shots from the back seat. One day, approaching dusk, we cruised into the wide main street of a small country town. It boasted the usual architectural fare: post office, police station, court house, bank, farm machinery yard, a church and a hotel. Ahead of us we could see the bright neon advertising signage of a service station and a well-known fast food restaurant, but it was too early to eat so we kept going. Such is the power of advertising that, as we passed the fast food outlet, a small disappointed voice belonging to a child who could not yet read, and who had never eaten fast food, asked, 'Aren't we going to stop for some fucky-eyed kitty?' We had to pull off the road.

FULL DISCLOSURE: THE BEST TRAVEL PLANNING ADVICE FROM WELL-TRAVELLED MOTHERS

If you can, avoid school holidays, both at home and at your destination.

✦

Scour weekend papers for special offers (e.g., kids stay free), and search for deals on airline and tourist information websites.

✦

Check services that airlines offer for babies and children regarding strollers, children's baggage allowance, baby bottles, infant food and in-flight entertainment.

✦

Most long-haul flights have bassinets for babies under a certain weight. They pull out from the bulkhead in front of you. Book seats and bassinet early.

✦

If you're having difficulty online due to patchy internet in rural areas, take the information you found to a travel agent. Many will match or better the price.

✦

Check passport, vaccination and visa requirements. Some countries require passports to be valid for six months after your travel dates.

✦

It is much easier and often cheaper if four people use taxis to and from airports rather than public transport.

✦

Check out university accommodation in major international cities. Some turf out students during holiday periods and tourists can book in. Most have clean, reasonably priced rooms in good locations, which can save heaps on city transport costs. This takes internet searching, but it's worth it. As always, read reviews.

✦

Travel insurance is strongly recommended. Travelling with young children is unpredictable. Even an ear infection can prevent a child from flying.

✦

If you are pregnant or travelling with a newborn, check cut-off dates with airlines. You might need a 'fit to fly' certificate from a doctor. Also, check if there have been any recent outbreaks of diseases at your destination that might place your baby at risk, e.g., zika virus.

✦

Check if the airline has a 'one adult to each child' rule. Some do and this means you need two adults to travel with two children.

TOP TIPS FROM MOTHERS ON FLYING WITH BABIES AND CHILDREN

Check with airline and airport security about the current regulations for taking liquids for bottle feeds, baby food, medications, nappy creams, etc. on aircraft.

✦

Regardless of what the airline provides for babies and children, assume they will run out and take what you need. Prepare for the worst – plane delays, fevers, etc. Take more nappies and wet wipes than you need and, if allowed, take your infant's favourite foods. Notify the airline in advance if you will need cow's milk.

✦

Smile at everyone in uniform and hopefully they will help you.

✦

Check-in takes longer with small children. If you haven't checked in online, ask if the plane is full. If it isn't, ask if you can be seated next to a vacant seat.

✦

Change your baby's nappy right before you board the aircraft.

✦

Most airlines allow you to use a stroller (make sure you label it) right up until you board. They give it back as you disembark. This is an invaluable service, as you can be hands-free to complete the departure and arrival tasks.

✦

Stay together as a family. You won't clear security with baby liquids if someone has gone ahead with a crying baby.

✦

Young children can get lost in airports. Label them with your name and phone number.

✦

Pack a backpack for each child with a change of clothes and things to amuse them.

✦

Take a change of clothes for yourself – you don't want to arrive smelling of Eau de Babysick.

✦

Have boiled sweets for small children to suck on take-off and landing. Feed your baby (either breast or bottle) on take-off and landing, as sucking helps equalise pressure in their ears.

✦

Take your baby's own familiar bowl and utensils.

✦

It's almost impossible to lower the baby change table in an aircraft bathroom while holding a baby. Ask someone to do it before you go in.

✦

Always ask for bottles to be heated before you need them. Flight attendants are busy and you may have to wait – not ideal if your baby is crying with hunger.

✦

If your baby is screaming and people are making faces at you, ignore them. Remember, you will probably never see them again. If you see another parent having problems with a baby or young child, ask if you can help them.

✦

Carry sets of earplugs to distribute to your neighbours if things get really bad.

✦ MEMO ✦

No matter how many horror stories you hear about travelling with babies and small children, it is nothing, repeat nothing, compared to travelling with teenagers.

MOTHER'S PRIVATE GOING-AWAY CHECKLIST (AND IT'S ALL ABOUT COMING HOME)

Organise for someone to clean your home while you're away – there's no point in returning to a dirty house and undoing good holiday vibes.

Before going away, buy wine or chocolates for the person looking after your post and plants – then that job is done and the gift is ready for you to give them when you return.

Put milk, bread and butter in the freezer ready to thaw on your return.

Have dinner for the first night home organised in the pantry or freezer – I've never met a frozen pizza I didn't like.

WARNING!

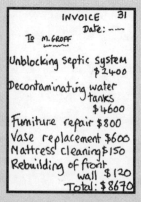

INVOICE 31
Date: ——

To M. GROFF

Unblocking septic system
$2400
Decontaminating water tanks
$4600
Furniture repair $800
Vase replacement $600
Mattress cleaning $150
Rebuilding of front wall $120
Total: $8670

Repair bills from free family holidays at a friend's holiday apartment or weekender will equal the NATO defence budget.

REVEALED: THE TOP SEVEN PACKING TIPS

1. Pack for seven days, even if going away for two months.
2. Make a list and stick to it. If you need something when you get there, buy it – it'll make a good souvenir. And take the list with you to tick off as you re-pack for home.
3. If flying, pack items or clothes that you can't bear to lose in your hand luggage. The same goes for precious toys and anything of value.
4. If renting a holiday apartment within your own country (don't take any strange powders abroad), pack small amounts of well-labelled washing powder, dishwashing powder, and a dishcloth and tea towels. Few holiday apartments supply these.
5. Pack things on top that will be needed as soon as you arrive at the destination – like swimming costumes, hats and beach towels.
6. Put everything into suitcases or bags, even tennis racquets. Loose items are a pain to transport and have more chance of being lost.
7. Label suitcases inside and out. I have lost and had returned suitcases that have travelled further than me.

DID YOU KNOW

If you are staying in a hotel in a freezing cold or sweltering hot climate, you can sometimes keep the power and air-conditioning on in your room when you go out (so it's a perfect temperature when you return with hot/cold/tired children) by slotting any plastic card (I use my library card) into the key card wall slot. But remember to place a Do Not Disturb sign on the door so housekeeping don't come in and take your card away.

REVEALED: THE BIGGEST MISTAKE PEOPLE MAKE WHEN TRAVELLING

Taking too much luggage! It can ruin a trip, that's how much of a mistake it is. For a holiday of seven days or longer, at the very most each person needs the following items (and you will obviously adjust it according to gender and climate):

+ 1 sarong (useful to wear, use as a towel, scarf or sun protection)
+ 2 pairs of shorts or 1 pair of shorts and 1 skirt
+ 2 pairs of long pants (1 jeans, 1 other)
+ 2 shirts
+ 3 T-shirts
+ 2 swimming costumes
+ 2 sweaters (or 1 cardigan, 1 other warm top)
+ 1 dress that doesn't crease
+ 2 hats (1 cap, 1 sun hat)
+ 3 pairs of shoes (walking or sneakers, flat dress and sandals)

In addition, pack for each person:

+ 1 lightweight rain jacket
+ 1 warm jacket
+ underwear/socks

Exemptions are packing for babies: always prepare for the worst. Make your own master list to cover sunglasses, cameras, sports equipment, books, etc. You can sleep in a T-shirt and undies.

THE HIDDEN PITFALLS OF STAYING WITH FRIENDS AND RELATIVES

Two main considerations:

How wild are your children?

✦

How fussy are the hosts?

If the answer to either is 'very', reconsider your plans. There is no sense in destroying friendships and spending a week with white knuckles. If you do stay, here are some tips:

Limit shower times.

✦

Hang wet towels outside.

✦

Purchase groceries – lots of them.

✦

Offer to cook and also take hosts out for a meal.

✦

Make your children clear away after meals – and have them offer to do other chores. You too!

✦

Purchase a thank-you gift.

And don't stay too long. Remember, houseguests are like fish – after three days they go off.

DON'T LEAVE HOME WITHOUT

Scanning all important travel documents, card and phone numbers, etc., so they are accessible in case of emergency.

✦

An external hard drive to back up all your travel photos (if you're not using your phone and saving photos to the cloud) and for working or writing when you're using someone else's computer.

✦

Copies of any prescriptions for medication.

✦

Spare prescription glasses and a photo of your prescription.

✦

Giving a neighbour your mobile number (or email address, if you are heading overseas).

IDEAS FOR THANK-YOU GIFTS

- ✦ a high-powered torch or battery lamp
- ✦ a toasted-sandwich maker
- ✦ an electric carving knife
- ✦ several top-quality beach towels
- ✦ a beach umbrella
- ✦ a board game
- ✦ a salad bowl
- ✦ a rubber-backed picnic rug
- ✦ a picnic basket
- ✦ a dozen bottles of great pickles
- ✦ a well-established rosebush
- ✦ a bread board

You shouldn't scrimp on whatever you buy. This may seem an odd list, but none involves the personal-taste problem. And they're all useful.

TOP CAR-TRAVEL TIPS

Your five-hour journey will take six.

✦

If you are travelling with a child who has afternoon naps, leave home just after lunch so they sleep for the first couple of hours.

✦

Know where public toilets are en route.

✦

Do not stop at a playground. Someone will knock a tooth out.

✦

Organise distractions – iPods, iPads, games, ebooks, DVDs, CDs and washable window markers. Carry spare batteries. For short journeys, bring water bottles and snacks that aren't sticky. For longer journeys, pack a picnic and stop to eat it.

✦

Take an empty throw-away container with lid, and washcloth or wipes for car sickness, as well as spare clothes and plastic bags.

✦

Keep a bag of chewy mints in the glove box for older children – no one can complain and chew at the same time.

✦

Stash bribes in the glove box for desperate times.

✦

Promise a treat on arrival and follow through.

*'Some cause happiness wherever they go;
others whenever they go.'*

Oscar Wilde

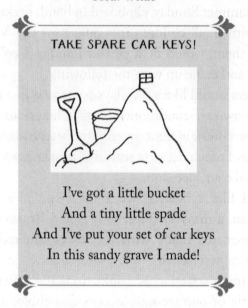

TAKE SPARE CAR KEYS!

I've got a little bucket
And a tiny little spade
And I've put your set of car keys
In this sandy grave I made!

THE UGLY TRUTH OF WHY I SPY
HAS HAD ITS DAY

Because children who like to play I Spy can't spell.

Example:

'I spy with my little eye something beginning with H.'
(Answer: GRASS.)

'It's my turn.'

'You've just had a turn.'

'No, I haven't.'

THUMP

'Mum!'

'SHUT UP!'

THIS WILL SURPRISE YOU, BUT IT'S WHAT MOTHERS WANT ...

One hot summer Sunday, clipboard in hand, I asked mothers waiting with small children in a queue for the Manly ferry what, for them, would be a perfect holiday. I collated their responses and came up with the following:

Mothers would like a few days every year in a quiet place with their own air-conditioned room, a luxurious bathroom, a complete entertainment system and gorgeous meals with stupendous French desserts served at set times so they never have to make any decisions.

They'd like a heated swimming pool, pleasant walks, a beautician, a masseur (preferably called Bruno or Dante), a hairdresser, tea made with tea leaves, filtered Brazilian coffee, room service, the best wines, a movie collection to choose from, a selection of books from the latest bestseller list, a bottle of outrageously expensive bubbles and a bowl of imported chocolates (none of that spring water and fresh fruit nonsense, thank you).

Rules as follows:

No children, no phones, no photographs, no visitors, no social media, no pizzas, no postcards and no questions.

Sounds divine ...

EIGHT

Children's Wingdings

The traditional meaning of 'wingding' is a lively party or celebration, as opposed to the modern meaning of dingbat fonts.

My mother always said the most important thing to have at our family wingdings was survivors.

GLOBAL WARNING!

A child's birthday party is way more than a birthday party. The event you organise, the thrills, new experiences and money you spend will demonstrate your level of financial success and cement your child's standing in their important social circles. And the moon is made of cheese . . .

✤ MEMO ✤

Don't let anyone tell you a child's party is easy. It's not. Adult parties are a breeze compared to the organisation involved in feeding and entertaining a group of four-year-olds. Remember to expect disturbed sleep the night before and an inability to eat breakfast, but you'll be fine by party time.

HELP! HOW MANY CHILDREN DO I INVITE?

This depends on budget, space, plans and whether you're partying at home, at the park or at a party-specific venue. Once you have decided how much to spend and where to hold the party, then work out numbers.

For parties at home, I only ever invited eight children in total. This was because I only had eight parfait glasses.

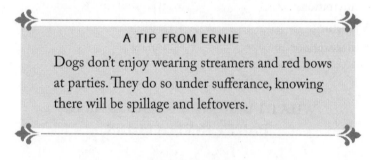

A TIP FROM ERNIE

Dogs don't enjoy wearing streamers and red bows at parties. They do so under sufferance, knowing there will be spillage and leftovers.

DID YOU KNOW

In some East Asian countries a baby is considered to be one year old the day it is born. If the baby is born just before Chinese New Year, when it gains another year of age, it can be two years old having only been alive for a month. The practice is common in China, Korea, Taiwan, Hong Kong and Vietnam.

TIME TO TAKE THE BIRTHDAY TEST

If you are unsure about holding a child's birthday party at home, repeat 'Put that down!' a hundred times to test if you're still keen.

THE ULTIMATE PARTY-PLANNING CHECKLIST

+ budget
+ day and date
+ time – start and finish
+ location – home or away
+ number of children
+ parents to stay?
+ invitations
+ theme
+ decorations/music

+ food
+ drinks
+ cake
+ entertainment and/or games
+ prizes and loot bags
+ refreshments for adults
+ parking
+ piñata

WHAT I LEARNED <u>SHOULD</u> BE ON PARTY INVITATIONS

+ your child's name and age
+ a message saying 'looking forward to seeing you at my party'
+ name of the invited child
+ a request to be advised of any food allergies
+ party location
+ date and day

✦ start and finish time, i.e. 11.30 a.m. to 1.30 p.m. sharp
✦ theme, i.e. pirates, fairies, fancy dress
✦ your name and contact details
✦ parking information, if required

TOP TIP (this is the wrong way round, but it works)
Before sending out invitations that will require an RSVP, call or text a parent of each child on your invite list and ask if their child would like to come. This gives you a good idea of numbers right at the start of planning. And if you think a parent should stay, say so. Contact ditherers a few days later. Once you know who and how many are coming, then distribute the invitations as a matter of formality and information.

SIXTEEN SMART AND SIMPLE WAYS TO SURVIVE A CHILD'S PARTY

1. Remember to focus on the children and their pleasure. This is a child's party, and not a competition between mothers. Oh okay, it is a bit, but it shouldn't be. The whole birthday thing has got way out of hand. I'm just saying . . .
2. Keep food and activities simple so that all children enjoy the party. If you have complex games and gourmet food, some children won't have fun. Go for the majority.
3. You are in charge, not the children.
4. Go mad with decorations and have children help. Twist streamers as you hang them. Don't skimp. The more the merrier. Hang balloons in bunches in the corners of the room.

Use coloured light globes to set the party mood – most balloons are made of natural rubber latex, but do not release them into the air.

5. Attach two balloons to the front gate. This starts the excitement rolling and lets parents know where to park.

6. Remove precious breakables such as porcelain and guinea pigs.

7. Hit the internet for theme ideas – pirates, Peppa Pig, disco, Star Wars, fairies and elves, the colour green, something beginning with 'P' – there are great ideas out there.

8. For young children, try to borrow small tables and chairs from a preschool. Four tables pushed together to form a larger square works best.

9. The table has to look great. Purchase themed party supplies – tablecloth, cups, plates and serviettes, or colour-coordinate it yourself.

10. Try to hire or borrow play equipment such as mini see-saws and mini climbing frames from local playgroups or preschools. Don't hire a trampoline unless you want to spend the afternoon at an X-ray department.

11. Annual parties too much? Nothing wrong with holding a party on alternate years and in between having a fun trip to the movies or zoo with a few friends.

12. Don't pick afternoon nap time for a party for young children. And two hours is plenty for a birthday party. One and a half hours is better – 11.30 a.m. to 1 p.m. or 12 noon to 1.30 p.m. covers lunch nicely and allows for a sleep afterwards.

13. If holding the party at a park, take account of potential weather problems, parking, shade, play equipment and access to public toilets.

14. Expect tears. It's their party and they'll cry if they want to.

15. A party isn't a party without music. But if children are too revved up and are going troppo, lower the sound and play Cemetery (see page 260).

16. A birthday cake with a spectacular sculpture on the top will be required – something simple, like a three-legged komodo dragon riding a skateboard that will take you four evenings to decorate. The kids will have one bite and then throw the cake on their plate and run off to play.

MARKETING THE DREAM

It is worth knowing (based on absolutely no research whatsoever) that children always have fond memories of parties held at home.

This is due to constant reminders – the carpet stain where Mark spilt cordial, the permanent gap in the row of peonies damaged when George (hi George, hope you're enjoying life in Florida) crashed through the flowerbed on his new tricycle, and the lawn where Olivia ate rabbit droppings because she thought they were currants (and I'm so sorry about that, Olivia).

Mostly, though, I think it's because children like to see you drilled into exhaustion with party preparation. They seethe with excitement when bags of balloons appear in the shopping, and just knowing that somewhere in the kitchen is a cake and candles and prizes is right up there with Christmas Eve. As with many things, slow anticipation is the most delicious part.

FOOLPROOF ORDER OF EVENTS

 1.   Children arrive/presents   15 minutes
2.   Food (savoury then sweet)   30 minutes
3.   Games   25 minutes
4.   Cake   15 minutes
5.   Loot bags to take home   5 minutes

Total   90 minutes

PERFECT!

THE BIRTHDAY PARADOX
(AMAZING, BUT TRUE)

In a group of only twenty-three people, there is a 50 per cent chance of two people having the same birthday. In a group of seventy-five people, the odds rise to 99.9 per cent.

INSIDER TIPS FOR USING PARTY SERVICES AND VENUES

Hop online to find local party services and party-specific venues:

Check minimum/maximum numbers required.

✦

Is entertainment provided? (Tip: young children are quickly bored by magicians and can be frightened by clowns.)

✦

Are food and drinks provided, and do they customise options for special diets?

✦

Is supervision provided or do parents stay?

✦

What is the price per head?

✦

Is there adequate parking?

LET'S HEAR IT FOR CLASSIC PARTY GAMES

You'll find lots of party game ideas with instructions online, such as an egg and spoon race (use chocolate eggs, and Blu Tack egg to the spoon for littlies), pass the parcel (everyone wins a prize with each unwrap), musical cushions, pin the tail on the donkey, a piñata, etc.

TIPS

Have a large bag of lollies in your pocket – hand one out to any child whose bottom lip is quivering because they haven't won a prize yet. This is no time for lessons on losing or life not being fair.

✦

Every guest should win at least one game. You will have to use incredible subterfuge and outrageous deceit to achieve this. The trick is to keep talking loudly so that no one can interrupt and dispute the umpire's decision.

✦

There is only one umpire. You. Other grown-ups might be too indoctrinated with fair play to understand the finer points of uncontrollable sobbing behind the bathroom door because Harper won the prize that Frankie wanted.

The same game can be played many times. These games are known to umpires as practice games and they are played until the completely inept child (because there is always one who couldn't fight their way out of a paper bag) eventually wins, at which point the turn is classified as a real game and the incompetent child claims their prize.

TIPS FOR PRIZES

If you see a good party prize on special, buy a dozen and keep them in a party box. Prizes don't have to be elaborate or expensive, just fun. Ideas: crayons, colouring books, gimmicky pens or pencils, pencil sharpeners, fancy notepads, sparkly shoelaces, sheets of stickers, playing cards, little trolls, big lollipops, etc.

ADVANCED TIP: Having identical prizes avoids punch-ups. But not always.

❧ MEMO ❧

If you are handing out balloons to small children when they leave, tie a length of gift-wrap ribbon to it and put a sweet inside the balloon before you blow it up. This alleviates tears if the balloon bursts. Of course, all other children will then burst their balloons . . .

THINK OUTSIDE THE BOX

If you have a work commitment, the family is moving house or someone is unwell, it's perfectly okay NOT to tell a very young child that it is their birthday. Save the news for later when things have settled down and you have time to enjoy your child's big day.

IS THIS THE BEST CHILDREN'S PARTY GAME EVER INVENTED?

Played in the garden or park, Late for School Race is a terrific game, but it takes preparation and a trip to a second-hand store. The rewards of children and parents helpless with laughter make it worthwhile.

Mark out starting and finishing lines on the ground with string. Children stand behind the starting line in a row. In front of each child, spaced out evenly between starting and finishing lines, are four items of old clothing or accessories, which will be their pretend school uniform.

The game clothes are put on over party clothes, so use bigger items as they are easier to put on. The first pile can be trousers or a skirt, the second an old shirt or T-shirt, the third old jewellery and the fourth a hat or umbrella.

Use an alarm clock to signal 'go' – it sets the mood. Each child must now run to the first pile and put on trousers, race to the next pile and put on the shirt, and so on until the first one dressed is over the finish line.

Mostly it's just a riotous heap of laughing children. It works best with over-fours. Don't forget to take a class photo at the end.

It's not just you . . . ten out of ten mothers at our
monthly mothers' lunches buy their own
birthday presents.

RISK MANAGEMENT

Whether you stay with your child at a party or just drop them off, remind them beforehand to say 'Happy Birthday' and 'Thank you for inviting me' to the host, and not to throw a wobbly when all attention is on the birthday boy or girl and they have all the presents.

There are big brownie points to be scored by being the mother of a well-mannered child. Yay!

WARNING! PARTY OVERLOAD

Once preschool and real school start, the party circuit kicks in. Your child might be invited to several parties in one weekend, which can really dig into family time, finances and other commitments.

TIP: From the get-go, decide how many parties your child will attend and make sure your child knows this. You can always make exceptions – and you will have to – for a relative's party.

WORRIED YOU MIGHT HAVE GONE A BIT OVERBOARD? DON'T BE . . .

In 1905 the American wine merchant and philanthropist George A. Kessler, also known as the Champagne King, held a memorable birthday party for King Edward VII at the Savoy Hotel in London.

Kessler wanted a Gondola Party so he flooded the hotel's central courtyard with enough water to float a large gondola (about 3 feet deep), built a bridge across to the gondola and erected scenery depicting Venice. The entire venue was then strewn with 12,000 carnations. Nothing over the top so far.

At the party, white doves flew overhead and costumed gondoliers served dinner to two dozen guests on the gondola while the world-famous Italian tenor Enrico Caruso sang to them. Then a baby elephant from London Zoo trotted over the bridge carrying a 5-foot-tall birthday cake on its back.

This amazing party was topped only by Kessler himself when he decided to have a North Pole Party at the Savoy.

TIPS ON GIFTS

Gifts your child takes to a party:

Keep a hidden stash of cards and presents. Stock up with four of the same thing if it's a good gift at a good price.

It's a nice touch if your child makes a card (strike one against materialism).

Ask the parent if there is a particular gift the birthday child would like. If not, you will be safe with books, movie tickets or gift certificates. Try to avoid plastic.

Birthday gifts your child receives:

If a parent asks you, make a suggestion, but always make it modest.

Rather than receiving a lot of tat, ask your child if they would like everyone to bring five dollars as a gift towards one good present of their choice. This is great. No tat. No wasted dollars. Everyone is happy.

You can recommend that your child asks friends to donate towards care of the zoo rhino, but you won't get anywhere. Excellent anti-materialism points for trying.

◆

If you mix in the higher echelons of society and there is a possibility of your child receiving a solid gold train set once owned by the King of Spain, then forget about the five dollar thing.

BIRTHSTONES AS GIFTS

Usually given as gifts for close friends or family, birthstones represent your month of birth. Although some months can have more than one gemstone, here is a list of modern and traditional gemstones from the International Gem Society.

January – Garnet	August – Peridot
February – Amethyst	(that's me, how dull!)
March – Aquamarine	September – Sapphire
April – Diamond	October – Opal
May – Emerald	November – Topaz
June – Pearl	December – Turquoise
July – Ruby	

IS THIS THE BEST, MOST ADORED, MOST VALUABLE AND MOST FAMOUS BIRTHDAY PRESENT EVER?

On 21 August 1921 a little English boy called Christopher Robin (nicknamed Billy Moon) was given a teddy bear from Harrods for his first birthday. Originally named Edward Bear, Christopher Robin later changed the name to Winnie the Pooh – Winnie after a Canadian bear of that name at the zoo in London, and Pooh after a swan he had named Pooh.

In time, Christopher Robin's father, British writer A. A. Milne, wrote stories about Christopher Robin and his toys Winnie the Pooh, Eeyore, Roo, Piglet, Tigger and Kanga. The four books became children's classics and have sold more than 50 million copies.

Today the value of the Winnie the Pooh brand is estimated to be in the billions. Apart from Roo who was lost in the apple orchard, Christopher Robin's much-loved Winnie the Pooh and his friends now live in Manhattan at the New York City Public Library where they have lots of visitors.

FULL DISCLOSURE ON DRINKS

1. There is nothing worse than preparing delicious fruit punch for young children who won't drink it. One will shout, 'Oh, yuck!' and the others will immediately chime in, the little dears. So don't bother, then you won't be upset.
2. Keep drinks simple. A large pitcher of homemade lemonade and one of apple juice will do eight children. If you run out, make Eskimo Specials – a glass of water with ice.
3. Don't serve pure orange juice. Excited, hot, full children can get one heck of a headache and throw up. I know this because . . . I just know it, okay.

❧ MEMO ❧

For parents who will be staying, prepare a simple cheese platter (one hard, one soft, one blue) with crackers, a bowl of mixed olives, a pip bowl, serviettes and a pitcher of iced tea.
Don't feel pressured to serve alcohol to adults – this is a child's party, not an excuse for a booze-up.

FINALLY: THE SECRET TO SUCCESSFUL PARTY FOOD FOR YOUNG CHILDREN

It's simple: follow the golden rule of three savoury platters, three sweet platters and one cake.

TIPS

Young children are conservative in their tastes so avoid unknown delicacies.

✦

Serve food that is easy to hold.

✦

Serve the three savoury platters first. When they are all eaten, serve three sweet platters.

✦

Remember, this is a party. Time for fun food and treats so one savoury platter and one sweet platter must be mind-blowingly spectacular.

✦

Prepare extra food as some parents arrive with gate-crashing siblings.

✦

As much as possible, prepare food ahead of time. And don't forget guests with allergies (their parent will stay).

✦

Do a practice run on party food recipes you plan to make yourself.

✦

Birthday cake is served after games. It is your grand finale!

SAVOURY SUGGESTIONS

You can buy savouries or slave over a hot stove – your choice. Children won't notice the difference and it's the presentation that is important: mini sausage rolls or mini pies with tomato sauce, dip and carrot sticks, small sausages, little sandwiches or mini quiche.

SWEET SUGGESTIONS

As with savoury ideas, if you are pushed for time purchase ready-made food: jellies, popcorn, mini cupcakes, iced doughnuts, chocolate crackles, fairy bread or fancy biscuits.

WHAT I KNOW ABOUT BIRTHDAY CAKE

There should be a law that mothers are discharged from hospital with one baby and one book on how to decorate birthday cakes. After all, most of us aren't going to make the cake. Like everything else to do with birthdays, it's the look that counts.

Whatever birthday cake recipe book you have, you can cheat on the cake-making part by buying ready-made sponge cakes from a supermarket and cutting them into the shape you need. Then pour yourself a drink and do your artwork.

TIP ONE: Over the years, I've found that five sparklers are just as impressive as twenty hours of laborious sculpting and icing.

TIP TWO: All birthday cakes should be hidden until serving.

FIVE FUN PARTY FOODS
(ALL RECIPES FEED EIGHT CHILDREN)

EASY MINI PIZZAS

You will need:

✦ *8 small pocket breads or similar*

✦ *tomato puree*

✦ *grated cheddar or mozzarella cheese*

Spread puree thinly onto pocket bread.

Sprinkle with cheese.

Grill until cheese has melted.

Cook just before party.

Allow one pizza per child.

NACHOS (for sharing)

You will need:

✦ *half a cup of tomato-based pasta sauce*

✦ *quarter cup of sour cream*

✦ *large packet of corn chips*

✦ *two cups of grated cheddar cheese*

Combine sauce and sour cream.

Spoon mixture over corn chips.

Sprinkle cheese on top.

Bake in medium oven for 10–15 minutes. Do this just before the party. It's fun and messy to eat – you'll have to show the children how to attack it.

FROGS IN THE POND
You will need:

+ *8 jelly dishes (glass ones are best)*
+ *2 packets of blue jelly*
+ *8 confectionery frogs*

Prepare one packet of blue jelly and pour into dishes to half-fill the bowl. Refrigerate and set.

Place one frog on each blue jelly.

Prepare next jelly packet and allow to cool before pouring over frogs. Refrigerate until set.

Make these the day before.

One per child is sufficient.

HARRODS BISCUITS
I call these Harrods biscuits because it's what I do when I want to make a fabulous thing even more fabulous – I say it's from Harrods.

You will need:

+ *1 packet of chocolate-flavoured biscuits*
+ *2 cups of assorted sweets (jelly beans, smarties, bananas, etc.)*
+ *1 packet of white chocolate melts*

Lay out biscuits on a tray.

Melt chocolate melts in a microwave oven.

When melted, spread over biscuits.

Now decorate biscuits with sweets, pressing them firmly into the warm chocolate.

You can do this the day before. Hide sweets until you need them. Then hide the biscuits until you need them.

STRAWBERRY PARFAITS

You will need:

+ *8 parfait glasses or similar*
+ *1 packet of strawberry jelly*
+ *1 packet of individual Swiss rolls*
+ *1 packet of strawberry dessert mix, plus milk as per packet instructions*
+ *300 ml of thickened cream*
+ *1 punnet of ripe strawberries*
+ *cocktail umbrellas for decoration*

Put one or two slices of Swiss roll in the bottom of each parfait glass.

Prepare strawberry jelly and pour over Swiss roll, just enough to cover. Refrigerate until set.

Prepare strawberry dessert mix by adding milk as per packet instructions. Pour or spoon over set jelly. Refrigerate until set. You can prepare to this stage the day before.

Whip cream until it peaks. Spoon onto parfaits. Decorate with fresh strawberries and cocktail umbrellas.

HOW TO TAKE THE PAIN OUT OF LOOT (OR LOLLY) BAGS

Ahhhhhhhhhhhhhhhhhhh!

I'm mildly confident that most mothers detest loot bags, but I'm totally confident that every child who goes to a party has been dreaming for days about the goodies in the bag and thinks loot bags are the most exciting thing in the world. So just do it.

Purchase empty loot bags from Kmart, kids' stores or look online.

◆

Buy two bags of mini Mars Bars, a bag of marshmallows, a multi-pack of fruit gum or pastilles, and a bag of Chupa Chups.

◆

Buy two types of small fun toys (not plastic) and two types of fancy stationery items from a discount store.

◆

Put eight items in each bag – two toy items, two stationery items, four confectionery treats.

◆

Put the same things in each bag.

◆

Secure the top with gift ribbon and label each bag with a child's name. Put them all in a basket ready for home-time.

◆

Give the loot bag to the parent who collects the child. And kudos for preparing spare loot bags for the guest's siblings.

SCHOOL DAY BIRTHDAYS

You've arranged a party for Saturday but want to do something on the real birthday which has fallen on a school day. If your school hasn't banned food-sharing or birthday cake, ask the teacher if you can deliver birthday cake to the school. If they say yes, ask how many children are in the class and add another portion for the teacher.

Most schools have a birthday-cake policy and parents of children with allergies should have already placed wrapped slices of cake for their child in the school freezer for when it is needed. If they haven't, you are not expected to make provisions for children with allergies, and as this is often a catering and emotional minefield it's sometimes best to abandon the cake idea and invite a couple of friends home to play after school and have a simple cake then.

If you are determined to send cake to school, and they let you, don't send anything that includes nuts of any type, or that requires the teacher to slice it. You will need to send a tray, paper serviettes, cake and a list of ingredients for the teacher to check. Simple cake ideas are best, such as individual cakes, mini-muffins or mini-cupcakes.

You can be an earthmother and make everything yourself, but children don't care if you've picked up cupcakes from the supermarket (but again, make sure the ingredients are listed on the package). It's quite amazing how caring you can feel delivering a tray of supermarket cupcakes to school. It's best to drop them off with the teacher in the morning and let them decide when to serve them. Your job is done!

NINE

Mothers' Secret Business

THREE IMPORTANT THINGS TO REMEMBER
BEFORE CHRISTMAS

1. 'I promise to walk it every day,' is a barefaced lie.
2. Producing rude noises with one's armpits is not suitable for the church Christmas talent quest.
3. Owning and breeding mice is not an essential memory of a happy childhood.

FOUR MESSAGES FROM SANTA

1. It is very rude for mothers to use the same wrapping paper as me.
2. If you don't have a chimney, you will notice that I sometimes leave a torn piece of red fabric snagged on a doorframe or windowsill. It's virtual reality; perception is everything.
3. On Christmas morning, as you stomp around clearing up the few dead leaves and branches that my reindeer have left on your floor, you should grumble about reindeer and disrespect for your carpet. It's called verbal authentication.
4. Lots of mothers ask me not to leave toys that need to be assembled on Christmas morning. They tell me they save those toys for birthdays, or ask me if I can have an elf assemble the toys before Christmas Day.

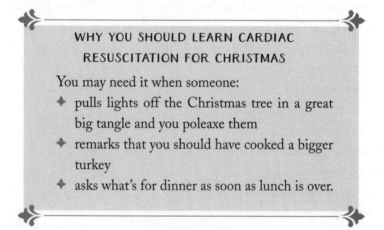

WHY YOU SHOULD LEARN CARDIAC RESUSCITATION FOR CHRISTMAS

You may need it when someone:

+ pulls lights off the Christmas tree in a great big tangle and you poleaxe them
+ remarks that you should have cooked a bigger turkey
+ asks what's for dinner as soon as lunch is over.

HO! HO! HO!

Mothers can happily keep the joyous excitement of Santa alive until an older child bursts the magic bubble, and this is never as traumatic and disappointing as you expect it to be. For many children the magic continues long after the reality hits – a fact which doesn't seem to bother them much, as evidenced by this long-ago conversation:

'Mum, you know Santa?'

'Not in the Biblical sense, darling.'

'Well, it's really Daddy, isn't it?'

'Of course not. Children who don't believe in Santa won't get any presents.'

'Okay.'

DID YOU KNOW

There is a town in snowy Alaska where Santa Claus lives and Christmas is celebrated 365 days a year. The town is called North Pole (but it's nowhere near the true North Pole) and Santa Claus rules from Santa Claus House, which is jam-packed with everything Christmas.

Local residents festoon their homes with permanent Yuletide decorations, and tourists flock to streets with names like Mistletoe Lane, Snowman Lane and Kris Kringle Drive. Even streetlights are designed to resemble striped candy canes.

It all started in 1949 when Con and Nellie Miller settled in Fairbanks, Alaska. Con, who was a merchant and fur buyer, liked to dress up as Santa Claus every Christmas for the children. By 1952, Con and Nellie had established a trading post in a nearby area called North Pole, and because Con was known as Santa Claus they called the trading post Santa Claus House. As the years went by the whole community became involved and slowly everything turned into Christmas.

In the lead-up to 25 December, some American TV stations broadcast from North Pole, and in the true spirit of the holiday season many Americans arrange for their Christmas cards and parcels to be posted from North Pole, just for the postmark.

LETTERS TO AND FROM SANTA

Many postal services across the world work closely with Santa Claus to make sure he receives children's letters and sends a response at Christmas.

Check on your postal service website for postage dates and Santa letter requirements. The local post office (if you still have one) might also display a dedicated Santa postbox. Don't forget to write your child's name and address on the back of the letter.

You can also type 'Letter from Santa with North Pole postmark' into your search engine and use one of the American organisations that will respond (usually for a fee) to your child's Santa letter with a genuine North Pole postmark. Alternatively, you can write the letter from Santa yourself, draw a postmark on the envelope and pop it in your own letterbox – for free.

SNEAKY STUFF: DO YOU KNOW HOW TO TRACK SANTA?

Today, thanks to special radar devices mounted on reindeer antlers, speedy satellites, high-powered telescopes, astronaut sightings and Santa-Cams, children can track Santa Claus on www.noradsanta.org as he and his reindeer fly around the world delivering presents to children.

NORAD is the North American Aerospace Defense Command, a joint American and Canadian organisation that has been tracking Santa Claus for over sixty years.

The story goes that back in 1955, a Colorado Springs store put an ad in the paper with a phone number that would connect children to Santa Claus. The misprinted number that appeared in the ad actually connected callers to the director of operations at the command centre now known as NORAD. And how amazingly lucky was that!

NORAD, who have been tracking Santa Claus to keep him safe in his global travels, have now declassified Santa's movements and can share his location with the world. Gee whizz, it certainly makes all those defence dollars worthwhile.

Children can also follow Santa Claus on one of his Twitter accounts – try @officialsanta or @santa.

A VERY PERSONAL CHRISTMAS STORY

Christmas is a time of great joy, though exactly who is experiencing the joy is not always obvious. It certainly wasn't joyous for me when, some years ago, I contracted food poisoning three days before Christmas. I was beyond caring about guests, but I managed to rally weakly and tell my husband that I had ordered a turkey and he was to collect it from the poultry shop at 6 o'clock on Christmas Eve. I remember falling back onto the pillow thinking I looked pale and interesting and saying, 'I've done it all. I've arranged everything. You go and enjoy yourself.'

It never occurred to me that this man who knew everything about me was unaware that each year I ordered a stuffed turkey from the gourmet poultry shop, which they also cooked, carved, reassembled and wrapped in double foil before I collected it on Christmas Eve. I assumed he knew that I reheated it the next day and pretended to have prepared the bird myself. I thought the Christmas Day praise was his way of playing the game.

Apparently not. At 8 o'clock on Christmas Eve he ran into our bedroom and announced in a panic, 'There's been a terrible mistake! Someone's given me the wrong turkey. It's all cut up and cooked and stuff. I've tried taking it back to the shop but it's shut. Oh God, Maggie, I'm so sorry.'

A sudden rush of adrenaline gave me the strength to sit up. My hands slapped my face in horror. 'Oh, no!' I wailed. 'Christmas is completely ruined!'

THE GRANDMOTHER AND THE TURKEY: A CHRISTMAS JOKE

A grandmother had invited all five of her children and their families for Christmas, so she set off to a nearby supermarket to buy a very large turkey.

But, oh dear, there were only small frozen turkeys left for sale. The grandmother looked for a shop assistant to ask about larger birds and found a young man who was working in the supermarket over the Christmas period. It was his first job.

Pointing to the small frozen turkeys, the grandmother asked, 'Do the turkeys get any bigger?'

The young man looked thoughtful and rubbed his chin. Eventually he said, 'No, they don't. They're definitely dead.'

NEXT YEAR, GO MAGI . . .

Those three wise men were on to something. Instead of truckloads of presents, many of which are made of plastic (and we aren't doing plastic anymore) and are discarded as soon as the wrapping paper is torn off, scale things back by only giving children three presents, one they want, one they need, and one to wear or read. This is in addition to a small stocking filled with fun stuff.

WORKING MOTHERS AND TURKEYS AGAINST CHRISTMAS

Please be advised that you are not alone if you love the idea of Christmas but find that:

✦ You start to dread the whole occasion as early as October.

✦ You loathe the exhausted, resentful person you become by the time it's all over.

You see, for many working mothers, the magic of Christmas has well and truly left the building.

THE NIGHTMARE BEFORE CHRISTMAS

During the lead-up to Christmas, mothers do any or all of the following:

plan and shop for presents for both their own and their partner's families

✦

buy wrapping paper and wrap the presents

✦

organise invites, parties and acceptances

✦

choose and buy Christmas cards, write the cards and letters and stand in line to post them all

✦

clean and tidy the house for the festivities

✦

shop for a less fortunate family

✦

organise the fridge and freezer so there is enough room for extra food

✦

stick cloves into an enormous ham

✦

steam Christmas puddings like Nigella, make mince pies like Jamie, bake a Christmas cake like Mary

✦

take children to see a comatose Santa at a shopping centre

✦

buy suitable festive clothes for an idyllic Christmas family photo, organise for aforementioned photo to be taken, distribute the photo via email and social media

✦

make costumes for the end-of-year school play, and attend the play

✦

take children to a Christmas concert and maybe the theatre

✦

prepare gifts for neighbours

✦

write cards and organise gifts for teachers

✦

find and buy advent calendars

✦

bake treats for work Christmas parties and attend the parties

✦

decorate the house

✦

drive interstate for the last toy animated dinosaur in the country

✦

plan, purchase and prepare all food for all meals during the festivities, including special meals for vegan, low-sodium and gluten-free diets.

During Christmas, mothers are on a constantly revolving turntable of:

clearing away mess

✦

phoning relatives

✦

texting greetings

✦

changing toilet rolls

✦

keeping bathrooms clean for visitors

✦

washing towels, tea towels and tablecloths

✦

preparing celebratory meals and clearing them away in time to start preparing the next meal, and on, and on, and on it goes.

PLEASE, SOMEONE MAKE IT STOP!

WHERE DID IT ALL GO WRONG?

Somehow in our march for women's rights, the question of who should be responsible for 'doing' Christmas was completely overlooked. As a result, we have exhausted mothers who still bear the load for creating the magic of Christmas; magic that was our mothers' and grandmothers' domain, except we are doing it all while working, as well as being on the receiving end of months of marketing pressure, forced expenditure of money we have worked hard to earn, incredible demands for culinary perfection created by endless cooking shows, and ridiculously high expectations from everyone.

While many men have stepped up to the plate, some haven't. They just buy the booze, pick up the tree and check what sport will be on television over Christmas. Meanwhile, mothers are being driven into the ground by this annual festivity, and the only celebrating they do is sighing with relief when it's all over.

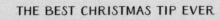

THE BEST CHRISTMAS TIP EVER

Unless you have a special family celebration that
involves decorating the Christmas tree, if you
have an artificial tree, think about leaving the
ornaments on it until the following year. Instead of
putting everything away, cover the decorated tree
with a large quilt cover, secure it tightly at the base
with string, and store it away until next year.

THREE WAYS TO OVERCOME THE CURRENT ORGY OF GREED AND MATERIALISM

1. Inform children that they will definitely receive something
    they want for Christmas (always open with the positive), but
    will receive fewer presents this year because your family will be
    donating money to an organisation that takes care of people and/
    or animals that need help. Discuss which charity with children.
    Set an amount and donate it. Tell children it is bad form to boast
    about giving to charity, although they may mention it if the need
    arises, and while you might inform your immediate family as an
    explanation of why you are not giving them all gifts, it's much
    better to keep quiet about it. *Noblesse oblige* and all that malarkey.
2. Make the children do some work. Each child has to really
    think about what they would like to give a sibling – you buy
    it, but they do the thinking and wrapping. As the old saying
    goes; it's the thought that counts. Hey, they might even want
    to make something.

3. Inform your parents and in-laws that this year you are combating materialism and would like the children to be given something they need, and advise what that is. Alternatively, say you would prefer that they receive a group present they can all play with, or that you would like them to have a special memory such as an outing to the zoo, a musical, or a theme park.

REVEALED: HOW TO ENJOY CHRISTMAS USING THE STAGGERING SCIENCE OF SIMPLICITY

1. If anyone asks whether you would like to go away at Christmas, say yes and start packing.
2. If you are staying home and have relatives and friends coming for lunch, plan the menu well in advance, make a list and delegate the workload to those attending. It's time to have the Christmas you want, not the ones you've had in the past. Nobody minds pitching in and most people love to be involved as long as they are told what to do.
3. Take shortcuts at every opportunity. It's your Christmas too. Buy the best mince pies, Christmas cake, Christmas pudding and all other culinary trimmings. Transfer everything to your own tins, containers and pots so it looks like you made it all yourself. I've been doing this for years. (Note to editor from Mrs Groff: Don't include that last sentence.)
4. If you are only a few for Christmas lunch, consider making a restaurant reservation – this can turn out to be cheaper than doing it all yourself. It's certainly more fun. Hey, you might even look half alive in the Christmas photos for a change.

5. Scale back the Christmas-card fiasco. Instead, write a humble, friendly Christmas letter with greetings and family news, maybe add a photo, and email it. Only send cards to people who don't use email, and include a printout of your Christmas letter. Otherwise it's a huge waste of your time and money.

6. Stop buying unnecessary gifts for the children of workmates, friends and neighbours, etc. And tell others to stop buying gifts for you and your children. There will be relief all round. If anyone calls you Scrooge or says 'Bah Humbug' you might smile and mention a charity donation. Or you might spit in their eye; it's your choice, depending on the sort of day you've had.

7. Many large families opt for an organised present-giving. Instead of everyone buying presents for each other, they put all the names in a hat, each person selects a name and then buys a really good present for that person. Set a decent price – don't be stingy with this. It's much better to have one great present rather than lots of crapola.

8. Some mothers have reported taking back Christmas by excluding the wider family and enjoying Christmas Day at home with their own family. This has allowed them to enjoy the children's excitement, take time with presents, play with their children, share the fun, prepare lunch and maybe go for a walk, teach their offspring how to ride bikes or roller skate, have a nap, or watch a Christmas movie together. Then they have a big family celebration a few days later. Now, there's an idea . . .

9. Grandparents have been known to go overboard with presents at Christmas and have been known to buy better presents than you or Santa. This happens. Get over it.

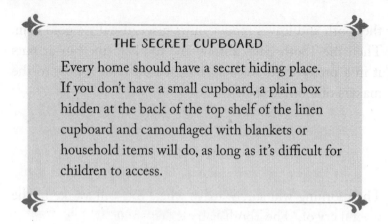

THE SECRET CUPBOARD

Every home should have a secret hiding place. If you don't have a small cupboard, a plain box hidden at the back of the top shelf of the linen cupboard and camouflaged with blankets or household items will do, as long as it's difficult for children to access.

THE EASTER BUNNY

Make magic bunny footprints (more virtual reality) to show the Easter Bunny has been:

Sprinkle patches of white flour on the kitchen floor.

✦

To make paw prints, press tips of your middle three fingers together, centre one on top.

✦

Tap paw prints in the flour as if the bunny has hopped across.

THE TOOTH FAIRY

In case there is someone out there who doesn't know how this works, when a child's tooth falls out, the tooth is washed and placed under the child's pillow when they go to sleep.

Sometime in the night, the beautiful Tooth Fairy takes

the tooth and leaves money in its place, usually a gold coin. Then the Tooth Fairy throws the tooth in the bin or puts it in a pretty tooth keeper, for a reason known only to the makers of tooth keepers.

OH, NO!

The morning will surely arrive when you will awake to the woeful cry of, 'The Tooth Fairy didn't come!'

Whoops . . .

You leap out of bed, race into your child's bedroom and grope frantically under the pillow while quickly and covertly depositing a coin.

You mumble reproofs like, 'Silly Tooth Fairy made it very hard to find.' Then you finally exclaim, 'Look! Here it is!'

The drama is over, but you are awash with guilt for this dastardly crime against motherhood. How could you?

TOOTH FAIRY INSURANCE

1. Place an emergency coin in a drawer beside your bed.
2. Place another coin in an unused mug on the top shelf of a kitchen cupboard.
3. Make a sign, 'Remember the Tooth Fairy' and tack it to the inside of the kitchen cupboard near the mug.

Method: When a tooth falls out, go to the cupboard, retrieve the sign and put it on the bathroom mirror where you clean your teeth at night so you don't forget. You have the coin ready in the mug. And you have back-up in the event you are too sick, drunk, upset or tired to clean your teeth, as you still have the coin in the drawer to grab in the morning. Smart, eh?

FAKING IT IN THE KITCHEN

'For the children's dinner tonight I'm making baby octopus stuffed with Icelandic figs followed by spring lamb roasted in coffee with a side salad of seaweed and raspberries,' said no mother – ever.

As you know, the food world has gone completely bonkers. Our homes are inundated with television shows featuring celebrity chefs and cut-throat cooking competitions, and everyone believes it's possible to cook Crepes Suzette with crème fraîche in under eight minutes on a windy hillside in Tierra del Fuego.

Mothers live, work and cook in the real world. We prepare meals for family members who are on a diet, who have just turned vegan, who haven't eaten since yesterday, who won't eat vegetables, who can't eat at all due to an affair of the heart, and for those who don't turn up for dinner, are late, or arrive home with three starving friends.

Unfortunately, courtesy of celebrity chefs, family members have come to expect a ridiculously high level of fine dining. There's only one way to address this unfair and unrealistic situation, and that's by cheating in the kitchen at every available opportunity.

It's time to embrace what I call Hoax Cuisine, a method of cooking that eliminates tiresome preparation by using top-quality prepared products. Many mothers already do this, but the secret to being a Hoax Cuisine expert is to hide the evidence and pass everything off as your own work. Yes, mothers, it's time to have a bit of fun – fake the bake and take the credit. Go for it!

WHO NEEDS HOAX CUISINE?

Hoax Cuisine is for busy mothers who want to enhance their domestic resume. It goes without saying that we all work too hard, and it's this pressure, caused by placing these unreasonable expectations on ourselves, that unites mothers – not fuzzy stuff about tenderness and giving birth to new life.

Hoax Cuisine will take you a step closer to domestic-goddess status without the need for tight sweaters. It will allow you to impress others with your bottled produce at the school fete, wow colleagues at office lunch parties, and see you elected as spokesperson for food issues at the World Health Organization (I may be getting ahead of myself here . . .).

SEVEN HOAX CUISINE BASICS

1. The main rule of Hoax Cuisine is to not let the people you're trying to impress know that you're doing it.
2. There's no point in passing off a store-bought item as your own if the foil tray is visible in the kitchen bin. After transferring

bought foods to your own containers, dispose of packaging in your outside bin, or even better, in your next door neighbour's bin.

3. Pickles, chutneys, sauces and salad dressings should be transferred to your own clean jars and bottles, labelled with your name and date, and refrigerated if required.

4. Deli produce such as sundried tomatoes and dips should be transferred to your own containers, labelled and refrigerated. Ready-made salads are usually in non-identifiable plastic containers and can be rebranded with your own label or transferred to a serving bowl.

5. Receipts should be destroyed or hidden, exactly as you do for new shoes.

6. Cakes, flans, pies and quiches from French patisseries and top-notch bakeries should be transferred to your own tins or dishes. Lining cake tins with greaseproof or baking paper lends an authentic touch.

THE BEGINNER'S GUIDE TO
A GOURMET KITCHEN

As it is with cubic zirconia and padded bras, perception is everything . . .

Display an attractive cooking pot, such as a Le Creuset, on the stovetop at all times.

✦

Purchase a bookstand upon which to display difficult recipes and pictures of wonderful dishes you have no intention of cooking.

✦

Stand a bottle of red wine next to the stovetop.

✦

Jars of your 'own' bottled produce should be on display.

✦

Hang a well-used and slightly burnt oven glove next to the oven.

✦

Grow herbs on your windowsill.

✦

Kitchen utensils in a pot should be highly visible next to the stovetop.

✦

Also next to the stovetop should be a basket containing a range of oils and vinegars.

✦

Hang a professional-looking chef's apron in full view – the blue and white striped jobs tick all the boxes.

✦

Purchase a large and spectacular wooden chopping board and keep it on the kitchen bench ready for no action whatsoever.

✦

Purchase a mortar and pestle. You won't be using these, but it's a good ruse to keep them on display so it appears you frequently pound exotic spices.

HOAX CUISINE
SKULLDUGGERY JAM

There's nothing like a jar of homemade jam to demonstrate your five-star cooking talents.

You will need:

+ an empty jar and lid
+ a jar of brand-name jam
+ an elastic band
+ a label
+ a calligraphy pen
+ pinking shears, or scissors
+ red and white checked gingham or similar
+ ribbon or a piece of raffia.

Wash and dry the jar – I use the dishwasher. Open the proprietary jam. Spoon the jam into your clean empty jar – you might have to chop at it a bit as some jam tends to be chunky and hard to settle. Screw the lid on.

Using the pinking shears, cut a circle of gingham fabric twice the size of the lid. Secure fabric over the lid with an elastic band and tie ribbon or raffia over the band.

Finally, use fancy writing to label your work – the date always adds authenticity. If your Skullduggery Jam is going to a community stall or school fundraiser, you'll have to copy the list of ingredients onto your label.

P.S. When talking to a radicalised earthmother, I have been known to say that I grew and picked the fruit myself.

TEN

School Daze

PRESCHOOL: USEFUL THINGS TO KNOW

An approved preschool may also be called other names such as an early childhood learning centre, kindergarten, nursery school, pre-primary, preschool playgroup and prep. They offer a safe environment and trained staff that provide 'structured' childcare with an educational leaning for children who are too young for real school.

There is strong pressure to send children to preschool,

particularly from profit-making concerns, but the cost can create financial pressure on a family. And trust me on this one – most people I know never went to preschool and were ready to attend real school when they were old enough to attend real school. That's why there are age rules.

At this stage, preschool is not compulsory and the decision to attend should be based on your child's needs, your family situation and personal choice. It's an option for working parents and for children who might benefit from early childhood education.

But playing imaginary games at home remains a preferred option of many parents until their child is old enough and ready for real school. In other words, preschool is your decision and don't be pushed into doing something you don't want to do.

WHERE IS THE WORLD'S OLDEST SCHOOL?

The University of Karueein in Fez, Morocco, is a co-educational, degree-awarding centre of higher learning. Also called Al-Qarawiyyin or Al-Karaouine, it was founded almost 1200 years ago in 859 AD and incorporated into Morocco's modern state university system in 1963, which, according to UNESCO and Guinness World Records, makes it the world's oldest existing and continually operating educational institution (although this claim is subject to question as the Zaytouna mosque-school in Tunisia was founded in 703 AD, but we'll go with UNESCO and Guinness World Records).

However, it isn't the overall age that is the most astonishing thing about the University of Karueein – it is that the school was pioneered and founded by a woman, Fatima al-Fihri, the visionary daughter of a wealthy North African merchant.

A LITTLE SCHOLASTIC HUMOUR

Mother: Son, get up – it's late!

Son: No! I want to stay in bed!

Mother (loudly): Get up NOW! It's time to go to school.

Son: But I don't want to go to school.

Mother (shouting): Get up NOW and go to school. You have to go. You're the principal!

AMAZING MATHS

12 + 1 = 13
11 + 2 = 13

AND

twelve + one is an anagram of eleven + two

GO FIGURE!

REAL SCHOOL

THREE THINGS TO KNOW

1. The first year of real schooling consists of learning through storytelling, counting, singing, reading, writing, building, painting and occasionally wetting your pants. It's a carefully constructed and smooth entry into formal education for children, whether they have come from a preschool or not.
2. The most important commodity in any school is the teacher. It's not mahogany desks, the latest technology, fancy school halls, famous alumni or fertile playing fields – it's Mr Chang with the elbow patches on his jacket and Ms Watson with the tremulous high-pitched singing voice.
3. Embarrassing your child is now a recognised art form. Kiss your child at the school gates and if that isn't working for you, wave frantically at them from afar and yell, 'Have a nice day, Snookums!' That should do it.

IS YOUR CHILD READY FOR REAL SCHOOL?

I was told by an experienced teacher that the benchmark for school readiness is social confidence and emotional development. Hmmm? I still don't know if I possess those qualities myself.

Let's pretend it means:

Your child is of eligible age.

✦

They want to go to real school and you think they are ready.

✦

You want them to go to real school and they think they are ready.

✦

You work and can't afford further childcare.

✦

Your child's friends are starting school.

And for goodness sake, if you have sent them too early and they are not coping, and they will still be within the legislated starting age the following year, TAKE THEM OUT!

WHERE IS THE WORLD'S MOST EXPENSIVE SCHOOL?

Not far from where I used to live in Lausanne, Switzerland, is the small town of Rolle, home to the marvellous Institut Le Rosey (or 'Rosey' as we called it), and reputed to have the highest school fees in the world. Situated on the edge of Lake Geneva, Rosey is a co-educational, bilingual (French and English) boarding school of 420 students.

There are two campuses, the main one at Rolle, which is on the site of a 14th-century chateau (of course it is), and a second campus in the mountains at Gstaad where students live in chalets and ski during winter months. Students comprise equal numbers of boys and girls from across the globe, and include royalty and the offspring of the rich, famous and powerful. (I, as you'd expect, lived and worked among the common folk.)

MY FIRST DAY AT REAL SCHOOL

It's etched onto my brain, next to first stitches and first fillings. I grew up in a house where people came and went with the tides. Grown-ups talked of storms in Bilbao, cargo in Valparaiso and the vagaries of the Suez Canal. I talked to my father on a ship-to-shore radio and listened to jungle tales of rubber-planting grandparents in Malaya. Imagine my excitement when finally, I, Maggie, was going somewhere, even if it was only to Castle Street County Primary in the village.

And so, one cold English morning, I was launched into the school system with a few stern words, bible-black shoes and a five-mile walk home. Indulgence and pampering were forbidden. Adversity bred fortitude and good character. Or so they said.

Then I met Charlie Bushell, age five. Charlie tied me to the school fountain with my skipping rope and told me that Reggie Two-Sticks, the wicked old man who lived on a boat at Portchester Castle, would come and eat me.

BEFORE YOUR CHILD'S FIRST DAY AT REAL SCHOOL

1. Register at the school and check starting date and uniform requirements, if any.
2. Attend the school's Orientation Day, if they have one.
3. Make sure your child's immunisations are up to date.
4. Don't harp on to your child about starting school. The less said the better.

5. Practise opening the lunchbox and drink bottle (your child, not you).

6. Label everything except your child with a black permanent laundry marker, even shoes.

7. Organise travel needs – bus pass and location of bus stops, bike chain and lock, car drop-off and pick-up areas, car-pooling options, etc.

If there are tears on your child's first day at school, be guided by the teacher. If the teacher says 'GO!', then go.

TIPS FOR YOUR CHILD'S FIRST <u>DAY</u> AT REAL SCHOOL

Allow an extra half-hour to get ready.

✦

Ignore tantrums. Let everything go this morning.

✦

Don't worry if your child can't eat breakfast. Unless there is a medical necessity, it doesn't matter. Put a bit extra in their lunchbox.

✦

Make a packed lunch your child is familiar with.

✦

Let them take a toy (put their name on it).

✦

Take your child to school and stay until the teacher tells you to go.

✦

Make sure your child knows the location of the toilets and water bubblers.

✦

Show your child where you will be standing at the end of the day. Try to avoid using after-school care and activities for the first week as they'll be tired.

✦

Don't stare at other parents having a bad time. Oh, okay. Just a bit.

✦

Find the location of the lost property bin. You will visit it regularly.

✦

Cry all the way home or to work. This is an emotional day. After dropping my daughter off for her first day of school I sat on a garden wall in Ben Boyd Road in Sydney and sobbed like a baby, wailing that I had abandoned my child to the Department of Education. I went back at lunchtime and looked through the gates. She was running around laughing and playing with other children, not a care in the world. My child wasn't missing me at all. So I cried again.

TIPS FOR YOUR CHILD'S FIRST <u>YEAR</u> AT REAL SCHOOL

Individualise the schoolbag with a badge or ribbon. Otherwise they'll come home with the wrong bag.

✦

A zipped clothing pocket keeps money safe.

✦

Put school clothes or uniform on AFTER breakfast.

✦

Pack spare underpants in a plastic bag in the schoolbag for accidents.

✦

If you can take a short time off work, ask the teacher if you can help out at recess – opening lunchboxes and drinks, encouraging nourishment and assisting the teacher to keep the children sitting down while they eat.

✦

If you have a regular weekday off work, ask if you can help in class with reading, or whatever the teacher needs. Volunteering in class will show you how your child has settled in, and will tell you more about your child's abilities than any school report.

✦

Helping in the school canteen is also a great learning experience. It's gossip central and you'll learn about all the other children in your child's class – and their families.

✦

At year's end, a note of appreciation to your child's teacher will mean a lot. Sending it via the principal is a nice sycophantic touch.

WHAT YOU SHOULD TELL THE TEACHER

If the home situation has changed, i.e. the death of a pet, a sibling to high school, a new baby, divorce, separation, a death in the family or moving house, etc.

All of the above can have a dramatic effect on a child's behaviour.

WHAT YOUR CHILD WILL TELL THE TEACHER

Oh, just about every personal secret your family has. The teacher will know if you drink wine every night, that you used the 'f' word on the phone, that Daddy has a relative who is in the slammer and that Nana has a leakage problem when she laughs.

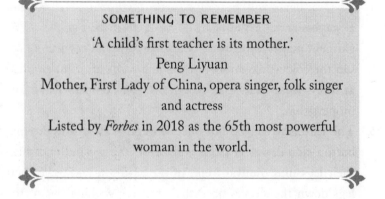

SOMETHING TO REMEMBER
'A child's first teacher is its mother.'
Peng Liyuan
Mother, First Lady of China, opera singer, folk singer
and actress
Listed by *Forbes* in 2018 as the 65th most powerful
woman in the world.

WHAT ARE COMPOSITE
(OR MIXED-AGE) CLASSES?

A composite or mixed-age class is a blend of students from two or more year levels of schooling. These classes are formed when there are too many or too few children from one year to make up a complete class, so they are amalgamated with one of the year levels on either side. Students continue to follow the curriculum for their normal year of schooling. They are not being 'put up' or 'kept down'. Composite classes are also formed for educational purposes when mixing age groups is considered advantageous.

TOP THREE USES FOR A SCHOOL CARDIGAN
HAND-KNITTED BY GRANDMA

1. The cardigan will be draped over high parallel bars and a succession of children will swing from the sleeves. The garment may now be worn by a young lowland gorilla.
2. On the coldest day in forty years, the cardigan will be traded at recess for a Mars Bar. It will later be dumped in the lost property bin.
3. The cardigan will be buttoned up and laid on the ground, button-side down. A child will lie on the ground and push their legs into the waist end of the cardigan and force their legs down the sleeves until their feet are sticking out of the cuffs. The child will then sit up and ask another child to pull the back of the cardigan over their head and back until their whole body is inside the cardigan and their head pops out of

the neck. They will then walk around like a ball on short legs. All school cardigans will be ruined on the day the first child learns how to do this. (You may wish to try this at home alone. It is very, very funny.)

WHERE IS THE WORLD'S LARGEST CLASSROOM?

Hang on to your hats! The Alice Springs School of the Air in the Northern Territory teaches primary and secondary school students in a classroom that covers 1.3 million square kilometres (502,000 square miles). That's ten times the size of England.

There are several schools of the air in Australia – in every state except Tasmania – as there are many remote areas of this vast country where there are not enough people to warrant a physical school being built. Since 1951 a significant number of children living in remote outback communities have been educated by Alice Springs School of the Air.

Lessons are taught by qualified teachers who follow the Australian education curriculum. Initially, lessons were delivered by a teacher to a student using two-way radio broadcasts. School materials, books and homework travelled between students in the outback and the teacher at the home base in Alice Springs via the Royal Flying Doctor Service, as some materials still do today.

With advances in technology and expansion of internet services, the School of the Air now uses satellite technology and Interactive Distance Learning (IDL), which allows transmission of data, audio and visual feeds as an adjunct to email, telephone and regular mail. Each student can log on to a teaching session, see, hear and speak to their teacher, and communicate with other students. After a teaching session, students usually complete assigned work at home with a parent.

Several times a year the students and teacher spend time with each other at home base in Alice Springs, and teachers also travel to remote locations to meet students and their families.

'EXPERIENCE IS A GOOD TEACHER, BUT SHE SENDS IN TERRIFIC BILLS'

There are many famous quotes about education and most are attributed to men.

However, the above quote is one of the all-time best and it's from an American mother and novelist, the late, great Minna Antrim.

WHAT IS A ONE-ROOM SCHOOLHOUSE?

A one-room schoolhouse is a school that consists of one classroom where one teacher teaches students of different ages at the same time. There were many such schools in sparsely populated and remote areas of numerous countries during the past two centuries. Over time, with an increasing focus on education, the one-room schoolhouse was often the first building established in developing communities. Academic basics were taught, younger children usually sat at the front, and the toilet was an outhouse. My husband went to a three-room schoolhouse in rural Missouri, and there are still one-room schoolhouses today in rural areas of several countries.

Although many one-room schoolhouses have closed and morphed into museums, some still operate in rural Russia, in remote areas and offshore islands of North America, such as Cliff Island, Maine, and in Scotland where the school on North Ronaldsay Island is 'mothballed' while awaiting new students since the sole pupil moved on to high school.

THE HELPFUL MOTHER: A SHORT TALE OF FAILURE

The first time I helped out at school was with reading at Neutral Bay Public School in Sydney. I took a group of five-year-olds into the playground and we sat on a bench under a tree and I read to them. Then they had a go at reading. At least, that was what was supposed to happen. All four children had ants in their pants and wouldn't sit still. They did everything to the bench except sit on it. By the end of page one there were only three children. I couldn't see Henry anywhere and I told the others to sit still while I searched for him. One of them promptly fell backwards off the bench and howled, and he took some settling down.

I can still see the teacher's face grinning at me through the classroom window as she pointed to the tree. I left Henry up there and suffered in silence as he dropped gumnuts on my head while I read. I tell you, I wouldn't be a teacher for all the tea in China. I improved as the years went by. I graduated to helping with embroidery and second place ribbon holder

on Sports Day. We don't speak about the school excursion to
Currumbin Wildlife Sanctuary.

THROUGH THE AGES –
TEN GREAT TEACHER MOVIES

Goodbye, Mr. Chips
(1939 and 1969)

The Corn is Green
(1945 and 1979)

The Children's Hour
(1961)

To Sir, with Love (1967)

*The Prime of Miss Jean
Brodie* (1969)

Stand and Deliver (1988)

Lean on Me (1989)

Dead Poets Society (1989)

Freedom Writers (2007)

The Class (2008)

AVERAGE ANNUAL INSTRUCTION DAYS OF
SECONDARY EDUCATION AROUND THE WORLD

(Numbers vary depending on locations within states
and countries, as well as pollution and weather
considerations.)

Australia	197	France	180	Israel	210
Canada	183	Germany	180	Italy	200
China	160	Greece	152	Japan	200
England	190	Hungary	180	Scotland	190
Finland	187	Iceland	170	USA	180

According to a 2014 Organisation for Economic
Co-operation and Development (OECD) report,
Australia has the highest number of compulsory
instruction hours per year: 10,120 hours.

ABSENTEE NOTES

The school needs to know when and why a student was absent. Depending on where you live and your school's requirements, you will have to either phone, text, email, complete details online, fill in a supplied form or pick up a pen and write a note.

A hand-written absentee note should include:

+ your child's name
+ their class
+ date/dates of absence
+ reason for absence – 'Jack was unwell' will suffice
+ if your child had an infectious disease, note this as well
+ your signature

Address it to the class teacher.

EXAMPLE
13th August 2019
Dear Ms Spicer,
Harry Dobson-Honey of 4S was absent from school on 12 August 2019. He was unwell. He is not infectious.
Regards,
Felicity Dobson (mother)

AND THEN THERE'S . . .
Hey Ms Spicer!
Harry didn't go to school yesterday, I expect you noticed. Ha!

We were at the hospital with his granddad because he had a stroke on the toilet and Grandma called an ambulance.

It turned out Granddad couldn't lift his left arm when he tried to stand up from the toilet because he had done up the button on his trouser fly to the buttonhole on his left shirt cuff. So he was okay.

The doctors thought it was funny. Grandma didn't.

Thanks,

Fizz Dobson

A

'To the uneducated, an A is just three sticks.'
A. A. Milne

WORLD TEACHERS' DAY

World Teachers' Day – also known as International Teachers' Day – is held each year on 5 October. It commemorates the anniversary of the 1966 International Labour Organisation/United Nations Educational, Scientific and Cultural Organisation Recommendation on the status of teachers. Oh, thank goodness we know that. Now we can get on with our lives.

LUNCHBOX TIPS

Butter sandwiches and rolls. Otherwise fillings fall out.

✦

Cut things in easily held chunks. Avoid unfamiliar foods (crappit heid), stainers (beetroot) and fruits that bruise (pears).

✦

Avoid over-wrapping by using a lunchbox with compartments, or put food in paper sandwich bags. Small containers will be lost. Cutlery will be lost.

❖

If your child likes a particular type of sandwich and it's healthy and nourishing, make it every day.

❖

Teach your child to use water bubblers.

❖

Tell your child to put used wrappers, apple cores, etc. back in their lunchbox. Then you can see what they've eaten.

❖

It will be reported back on day one that all other children have cola, chips and chocolate for lunch, and that their mother lets them buy an ice-block from the canteen. Oh, really? Worth a try, I suppose.

❖

Beware of giving treats. A young child with a lunchbox regularly filled with delicious booty is a sitting duck for older children with no consciences. Save treats for birthdays.

THE LIFE AND TIMES OF A SCHOOL LUNCHBOX

Food is eaten before morning bell.

❖

Lunchbox comes home unopened.

❖

Contents are removed from wrappers, bruised and left uneaten.

❖

Your homemade muesli slice is traded for chips.

✦

Contents come home untouched but box now contains leaves and grated rubber from beneath playground equipment.

✦

Contents come home untouched. Milky Way wrappers in child's pocket.

✦

Lunchbox is empty but child is starving.

✦

Lunchbox contains remains of someone else's sandwich.

✦

Lunchbox comes home with tadpoles swimming in it (I kept that lunchbox for years).

✦

Lunchbox does not come home.

Lost, stolen or strayed,
Benjamin Barlow's lunchbox
seems to have been mislaid.

LEFT- OR RIGHT-HANDED,
OR BOTH?

Most people in the world are right-handed. Ten per cent of people are left-handed, and more men are left-handed than women. One per cent of people are 'mixed-handed', i.e. they do some tasks with their left hand and other tasks with their right hand. Ambidexterity is when a person can use both hands equally well for everything. It is rare, and it can be learned.

HIGH SCHOOL: THINGS TO KNOW

All homework was due in last Monday.

Watching late-night television documentaries about sex is not a core component of the biology curriculum.

'It's at school' is a euphemism for 'I've lost it'.

Drawing genitalia in the dirt on the back of a teacher's car is not a sign of artistic talent.

The punishment for criticising your child's school friends is rubbish on the floor around the kitchen bin.

It's a criminal offence to emigrate while your child is at boarding school or school camp. No charges will be laid for thinking about it though.

HOMEWORK

Homework is every parent's nightmare. I would ban homework if I could. And there is evidence to support my view.

Finland is consistently named as having one of the best education systems in the world, if not *the* best, by many international groups. Finnish students do minimal homework, schooling is not compulsory until age seven, schools have no standard tests except one exam at the end of senior year, and educators (not politicians) make teaching decisions in education departments.

According to the Organisation for Economic Co-operation and Development (OECD), Finland is a top-performing OECD country in reading literacy, maths and sciences.

The dog ate my homework
has been upgraded to
Grandma deleted my homework.

HOMEWORK TIPS

The first bout of homework can really upset young children. They have heard bad stories about it, probably from me. Expect nightmares.

✦

It's essential to help in the early years – it's a barometer of your child's progress. And it gets it out of the way faster.

✦

During high school years you need to know what has to be done and when it has to be done by. Then you have to remind them every day for six or seven years.

✦

If your child needs tutoring, try to share a tutor with another student to reduce costs.

MOTHER'S GRAMMAR CRAMMER

A NOUN is the name of any thing
as **school** or **garden**, **hoop** or **swing**.
A PRONOUN stands instead of a noun
as **she** instead of Brenda Brown.
A VERB tells us of anything done
as **jump** or **skip** or **fly** or **run**.
An ADVERB tells how, why, when or where
as he travelled **behind** and she sat **there**.
An ADJECTIVE the noun describes
as **pretty** flowers or **clever** scribes.
A PREPOSITION stands before the noun,
as **in** or **through** the door.
CONJUNCTIONS join the words together
as men **and** women, wind **or** weather.
INTERJECTION shows surprise
as **Oh!** How pretty. **Ah!** How wise.

Author Unknown

SNEAKY HOMEWORK STRATEGY

I discovered this strategy by accident. It worked for me; I hope it works for you.

PROBLEM
As the middle-person between teacher and student it is often the mother, not the teacher, who becomes the mean and nasty homework ogre. As soon as homework comes through the front door the ball is in your court. You end up in the stressful situation of constantly nagging children to do homework, and in return you receive unpleasant backlash.

ACTION
Remove yourself from the middle by making it clear to your child that the giving of homework is the school's decision, and there is nothing you can do about it. Also, make it clear you will help if you can.

RESULT
Your child has no ammunition to fire at you when you give them a gentle reminder to do their homework, or ask if it has been done. Very quickly, your child should realise that homework is their responsibility, not yours.

TOP FIVE PLACES WHERE PRIMARY SCHOOL STUDENTS DO HOMEWORK

1. The kitchen bench, close to assistance.
2. The back seat of the car.
3. Grandma's dining-room table.
4. A waiting room at the doctor's surgery.
5. The floor beside your desk at work/home.

EDUCATION-SPEAK

Education departments across the world thrive on bureaucratic gobbledygook. The following phrases might help you to decipher official blurb from the school office:

'Simulated behavioural feedback': returning a student's disgusting drawing

◆

'Responsive performance models': gym equipment

◆

'Adaptive environment': demountable classrooms

◆

'Diagnostic learning systems': tests

◆

'Interactive instructional monitoring': teaching

◆

'Diagnostic student accountability': who did this?

◆

'Computer-based performance evaluation': school reports

◆

'Individualised teaching feedback': homework

✦

'Multi-dimensional behavioural management': punishment

✦

'Prescriptive performance environment': the playground

✦

'Collective educational models': teaching staff

✦

'Multi-responsive environmental manager': school caretaker

✦

'Individualised artistic expression': graffiti

✦

'Masticated mineral deposits': chewing gum

✦

'Visual analysis feedback studio': school library

✦

'Spontaneous instructional indicator': school bell

✦

'Quantitative density formula': the number of students per class

TOP FIVE PLACES WHERE HIGH SCHOOL STUDENTS SAY THEY DO THEIR HOMEWORK

1. In the school library.
2. At a friend's home.
3. In their bedroom.
4. On the school bus.
5. They don't do it at all because they are having fun on their phones/laptops/skateboards.

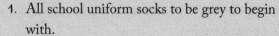

FIVE MORE THINGS MOTHERS WANT

1. All school uniform socks to be grey to begin with.
2. More respect for teachers and the teaching profession from politicians. Students hear constant derision of education standards in the lead-up to elections and it damages students' respect for their teachers and schools.
3. School grounds and sports facilities to be open for use during school holidays.
4. School canteens to serve containers of diced fresh fruit (some already do).
5. Homework questions to be clear and unambiguous.

SCHOOL HOLIDAYS

FOUR THINGS I HAVE BEEN TOLD MOTHERS MUST NOT DO DURING SCHOOL HOLIDAYS

1. It is very rude to complain to a friend about your child being home during school holidays while they are standing next to you. Apparently.
2. Never say, 'Would you like to go to the park?' One child will shout, 'Whoopee!' and two will turn their noses up. Say firmly, 'We are going to the park in one hour,' and follow this by asking them to sweep the kitchen floor. They will promptly disappear without argument.
3. Don't ruin your day by expecting teenagers to look as if they

are enjoying themselves. Let them sit well away from you at the beach. Sulking breeds character.

4. 'How long will you be gone?' is an improper response to, 'I've got great news!'

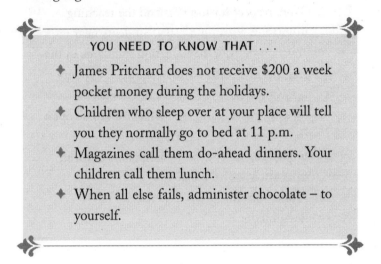

YOU NEED TO KNOW THAT . . .

✦ James Pritchard does not receive $200 a week pocket money during the holidays.

✦ Children who sleep over at your place will tell you they normally go to bed at 11 p.m.

✦ Magazines call them do-ahead dinners. Your children call them lunch.

✦ When all else fails, administer chocolate – to yourself.

EMERGENCY PLAYDOUGH

You will need:
✦ ½ cup plain flour
✦ ¼ cup salt
✦ 2 teaspoons cream of tartar
✦ 2 teaspoons cooking oil

Mix everything together. Add a few drops of food colouring to ⅓ cup boiling water, then combine with mixture. Allow to cool a little and knead the dough until smooth.

Then build to scale a brontosaurus (and let me know if you can figure out how to keep the head and neck raised. My brontosaurus always looked like a drunk. I had much better luck with stegosaurus.)

AN EMERGENCY PICNIC

Chaos reigns at home and you need to take the squabbling youngsters to a big space like Alaska, but the park will do. Pack butter, salad dressing, salad bowl, paper plates, cups, cutlery, breadboard, carving knife and drink requirements. On the way to the park, pick up the following from a supermarket:

+ cooked chicken
+ French loaf (baguette)
+ watermelon
+ ice (if you need it)
+ salad (cherry tomatoes, cucumber, pre-washed lettuce leaves, etc.)

+ ready-made potato salad
+ tub of olives
+ cheese (brie or camembert)
+ a dip

SMART PLANNING STRATEGIES FOR SURVIVING THE SCHOOL HOLIDAYS

Some children never get bored and are perfectly happy to tag along with daily life, play with friends and siblings, read books and go on an occasional outing. Then there are the others ...

> Draw up contingency plans before the holidays. These plans are not set in concrete, but they are there if you need them so you are not at the mercy of weather, sickness, bored children, other people, blocked drains or a broken head gasket in the car.

✦

Have your hair done so you won't look a fright in the window seat at McDonald's, and make sure you have one decent outfit ready in case of spur-of-the-moment invitations.

✦

Find out which school friends will be around for playdates and sleepovers and make a list of things to do. You may not end up doing any of it, but it's handy to be prepared when your brain is fried and someone asks, 'What are we doing today?'

✦

Google or call local tourist attractions, skating rinks, whatever you *might* do, and look up costs, hours, hire fees, etc. Bookmark the websites, or write it all down.

✦

Fill the fridge and pantry and make sure you have the doings for an impromptu family of five coming to lunch or a BBQ.

✦

If you plan on having a picnic you'll need to know where to go, so scout around your locale for picnic places that have shade, a table and seating, and are near play equipment and toilets, but not near a cliff edge or water.

✦

Make a list of potential wet-weather activities, such as putting up a tent in the garage, inviting school friends over to play on the firm understanding that their parents will reciprocate, holding a disco by pulling curtains closed and blasting the woofers and tweeters, making pizzas and muffins, throwing a spur-of-the-moment party (this will make you popular and well in credit with IOUs), making popcorn and watching movies . . . you know the drill.

HOW TO PLAY CEMETERY

Forget old hat games like snakes and ladders and chess and learn the brilliant new participant sport:

CEMETERY!

Everyone, except you, has to lie on the floor and pretend to be dead. The child who stays still the longest is the winner.

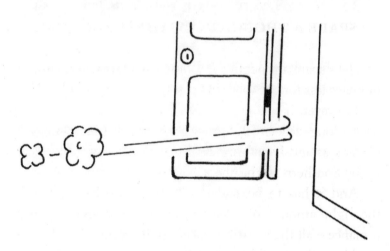

'WHO DID THIS?'

is the international evacuation signal for everyone under ten.

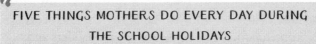

FIVE THINGS MOTHERS DO EVERY DAY DURING THE SCHOOL HOLIDAYS

1. Look out of the window first thing in the morning to check the weather.
2. Shout, 'Use a plate!'
3. Become suspicious when children are silent, and rush to see what they are up to.
4. Mutter, 'I just cleaned that.'
5. Wonder if it's too early for wine.

SPARE A THOUGHT FOR THESE MOTHERS

Yes, let's spare a thought for mothers in Italy where summer holidays last for between thirteen and sixteen weeks.

However, if you are a student it must be wonderful to have a long clear break from school that isn't interrupted by Christmas and New Year festivities, as summer holidays are in the Southern Hemisphere.

And it has to be said that thirteen weeks is probably the right amount of time to conduct a summer teenage romance – all the way from meeting to break-up.

Those thoughtful Italian educators!

THE MUMMY LIST

This is the fun part of school holidays where you plan activities for the first week back at school – for yourself. Whether you're a full-time mother, have worked through the holidays, or have taken time off and will be going back to work, try to have one or two days off and treat yourself to some mummy rewards: have lunch with a friend and only eat desserts, lie down at the beach instead of having to count heads in the water, go to an art gallery or museum and look at things in your own time, play golf, go horseriding – whatever floats your boat.

My favourite post-holiday treat was going to a department store with a friend and trying on expensive designer clothes; things I'd never wear and couldn't possibly afford. And I took photos. It's how I planned to do my publicity shots way back when my first book was published, but I looked tragic in the photographs. In hindsight, it's obvious the top designers never worked with a real woman wearing sneakers.

The other thing I loved to do was simply potter about the house, and if anyone out there needs someone to teach pottering at university level, I'm your girl.

HANDS UP IF YOU THOUGHT MARIA MONTESSORI WAS A TEACHER

Maria Montessori was the creator of the educational system known as the Montessori Method. Born in Italy in 1870, Montessori was the first woman to graduate as a doctor of medicine in Italy. Later, while working as a psychiatrist in Rome with children who had intellectual disabilities, she became interested in education and decided that, given the right environment and simple materials, the children could basically teach themselves through play and observation.

Based on this ideology, and embracing her strong conviction that children of normal intelligence would also self-educate if they were allowed to use their own initiative, in 1907 Dr Montessori opened her first preschool, the wonderfully named Casa dei Bambini, in a slum area of Rome. The simple materials she utilised were items such as beads, small slabs of wood and a series of cylinders.

Dr Montessori's teaching method proved enormously successful and led to her travelling through Europe, India and the United States of America giving lectures and establishing teacher-training programs. In time, Montessori schools were opened across the world – there are now more than 20,000.

THE FINAL WORDS

The final words on the subject of school should come from H. G. Wells who wrote the novel *Kipps: The Story of a Simple Soul.*

I studied *Kipps* at high school. I didn't enjoy the story, but there was a beautiful description in the book relating to school that has stayed with me all my life. When recalling a memory of his boyhood, Kipps relates that the school holidays 'shone like strips of stained-glass window in a dreary waste of scholastic wall'.

PERFECT.

NOTES

One: Oh, Mother!

DNA
Laura Geggel, 'Humanity Has More Mothers Than Fathers, DNA Reveals', *Live Science*, www.livescience.com/47976-more-mothers-in-human-history.html, accessed 30 June 2019.

Children should be seen and not heard
Phrases.org.uk, 'The Meaning and Origin of the Expression: Children Should Be Seen and Not Heard', www.phrases.org.uk/meanings/children-should-be-seen-and-not-heard.html, accessed 30 June 2019.

Invention of the bra
It was a hoax perpetrated by Wallace Reyburn in his 1971 book entitled *Bust-Up: The Uplifting Tale of Otto Titzling and the Development of the Bra* (London: Macdonald and Co., 1971); David Mikkelson, 'Brassiere and Otto Titzling: Was the Brassiere Invented by Otto Titzling?', Snopes.com, 19 May 2011, www.snopes.com/fact-check/bust-up/, accessed 30 June 2019.

Herminie Cadolle
Cadolle, 'Our Story', www.cadolle.com/en/content/14-our-story, accessed 30 June 2019.

Katharine McCormick

American Experience, 'The Pill: Katharine Dexter McCormick 1875-1967', www.pbs.org/wgbh/americanexperience/features/pill-katharine-dexter-mccormick-1875-1967/, accessed 30 June 2019.

Lucille Ball

Phil Dyess-Nugent, Erik Adams, Ryan McGee, Emily Todd VanDerWerff, Donna Bowman, and Genevieve Koski, AV CLUB: More than 60 years ago, a pregnant Lucille Ball couldn't call herself "pregnant" 24 July 2013 https://tv.avclub.com/more-than-60-years-ago-a-pregnant-lucille-ball-couldn-1798239435

Ancient Roman graffiti

Pomeiana.org, 'Graffiti from Pompei', compiled by Professor Brian Harvey (original authors unknown!), www.pompeiana.org/Resources/Ancient/Graffiti%20from%20Pompeii.htm, accessed 30 June 2019.

Albert Einstein quote

Christina Sterbenz, '12 Famous Quotes That Always Get Misattributed', *Business Insider Australia*, 8 October 2013, www.businessinsider.com.au/misattributed-quotes-2013-10, accessed 30 June 2019.

Two: Hello New Mothers, Wherever You Are!

Only 5 per cent of babies are delivered on time

Lauren Picker, 'The Truth About Due Dates', Parents.com, 11 June 2015, www.parents.com/pregnancy/giving-birth/labor-and-delivery/the-truth-about-due-dates/, accessed 3 July 2019.

Breastfeeding: the Papyrus Ebers
M. Papastavrou, S.M. Genitsaridi, E. Komodiki, S. Paliatsou, R. Midw et al. (2015) 'Breastfeeding in the Course of History', *Journal of Pediatrics and Neonatal Care* 2(6), https://medcraveonline.com/JPNC/JPNC-02-00096.pdf, accessed 3 July 2019.

Lotus birth
Lotus Birth.net, 'Lotus Birth: A Natural Birthing Practice', www.lotusbirth.net, accessed 30 June 2019.

Placentophagy
National Centre for Biotechnology Information, US National Library of Medicine, 'Notes on Placentophagy', www.ncbi.nlm.nih.gov/pmc/articles/PMC1807646/, accessed 30 June 2019; Cynthia W. Coyle, Kathryn E. Hulse, Katherine L. Wisner, Kara E. Driscoll and Crystal T. Clark, 'Placentophagy: Therapeutic Miracle or Myth?', *Archives of Women's Mental Health*, October 2015, Volume 18, Issue 5, www.ncbi.nlm.nih.gov/pmc/articles/PMC4580132/, accessed 3 July 2019.

Placenta rituals
Sir James Frazer, *The Golden Bough: A Study in Magic and Religion* (3rd edition), (London: Macmillan, 1890), specifically Chapter 9: 'The Worship of Trees'; E. Croft Long, 'The Placenta in Lore and Legend', *Bulletin of the Medical Library Association*, April 1963, 51(2), pp. 233–41, PMCID: PMC197976, https://www.ncbi.nlm.nih.gov/pmc/articles/PMC197976, accessed 24 July 2019.

Breastfeeding: The World Health Organization
World Health Organization, 'Breastfeeding', www.who.int/topics/breastfeeding/en/, accessed 30 June 2019.

Breastfeeding in France

Australian Government, Department of Health, 'France – The WHO Code and Breastfeeding: An International Comparative Overview', 3 May 2012, www1.health.gov.au/internet/publications/publishing.nsf/Content/int-comp-whocode-bf-init~int-comp-whocode-bf-init-ico~int-comp-whocode-bf-init-ico-france, accessed 30 June 2019.

Three: Troubleshooting for Mothers

Thumb sucking

J. Gillis, 'Bad Habits and Pernicious Results: Thumb Sucking and the Discipline of Late Nineteenth Century Paediatrics', *Medical History*, January 1996, 40(1), www.ncbi.nlm.nih.gov/pubmed/8824677#, accessed 3 July 2019.

Sigmund Freud on thumb sucking

International Dictionary of Psychoanalysis via Encyclopedia. com, 'Sucking/Thumbsucking', www.encyclopedia.com/psychology/dictionaries-thesauruses-pictures-and-press-releases/sucking thumbsucking, accessed 3 July 2019.

How the bowel works

Museum of Old and New Art (MONA), 'Cloaca Professional, 2010, Wim Delvoye' https://mona.net.au/stuff-to-do/monanism/cloaca-professional-2010, accessed 3 July 2019; Georgie Burgess, 'How MONA's 'Poo Machine' Became Enlisted in the Fight Against Bowel Cancer', ABC News, 8 November 2017, www.abc.net.au/news/2017-11-07/mona-poo-machine-joins-bowel-cancer-fight/9125910, accessed 3 July 2019.

Groom of the Stool

Ben Johnson, 'Groom of the Stool', Historic UK, www.historic-uk.com/HistoryUK/HistoryofBritain/Groom-of-the-Stool/, accessed 3 July 2019.

Teenagers with street cred

Peter F. Dorman, '**Tutankhamun**', Encyclopaedia Britannica, last updated 27 August 2019, www.britannica.com/biography/Tutankhamun, accessed 31 August 2019; Yvonne Lanhers and Malcolm G.A. Vale, '**Saint Joan of Arc**', Encyclopaedia Britannica, last updated 26 May 2019, www.britannica.com/biography/Saint-Joan-of-Arc, accessed 3 July 2019; the editors of Encyclopaedia Britannica, '**Catherine Howard**', Encyclopaedia Britannica, last updated 28 June 2019, www.britannica.com/biography/Catherine-Howard, accessed 3 July 2019; Kathleen Kuiper, '**Mary Wollstonecraft Shelley**', Encyclopaedia Britannica, last updated 8 May 2019, www.britannica.com/biography/Mary-Wollstonecraft-Shelley, accessed 31 August 2019 and Jill Lepore, 'The Strange and Twisted Life of "Frankenstein"', *The New Yorker*, 12 and 19 February, 2018, www.newyorker.com/magazine/2018/02/12/the-strange-and-twisted-life-of-frankenstein, accessed 3 July 2019; the editors of Encyclopaedia Britannica, '**Bobby Fischer**', Encyclopaedia Britannica, last updated 16 May 2019, www.britannica.com/biography/Bobby-Fischer, accessed 3 July 2019; Michael Berenbaum, last updated 18 June 2019, '**Anne Frank**', Encyclopaedia Britannica, www.britannica.com/biography/Anne-Frank, accessed 3 July 2019.

Four: Back to the Paid Workforce

Anna Fisher

Space Center, Houston, 'Astronaut Profile: Dr Anna L. Fisher' https://spacecenter.org/wp-content/uploads/2019/04/Anna-Fisher-Bio-Card-web.pdf, accessed 3 July 2019; and the video she is quoted from 'First Mom in Space! Anna Fisher Tells Her Amazing NASA Story | Video', www.youtube.com/watch?v=JWwfpfAjvco, accessed 3 July 2019.

Marriage bar and countries where women are restricted from work

Johnny Wood, '104 Countries Have Laws That Prevent Women from Working in Some Jobs' World Economic Forum, 13 August 2018, www.weforum.org/agenda/2018/08/104-countries-have-laws-that-prevent-women-from-working-in-some-jobs/, accessed 3 July 2019.

Shopping on Wednesday

Adam Bluestein, '29 Things Your Grocer Won't Tell You', www.rd.com/health/healthy-eating/13-things-your-grocer-wont-tell-you-slideshow/, accessed 3 July 2019.

Five: Order in the House

Mark Twain in Elmira

Centre for Mark Twain Studies, Elmira College, 'Quarry Farm', https://marktwainstudies.com/about/quarry-farm/, accessed 3 July 2019.

An Englishman's home is his castle

The Phrase Finder, 'The Meaning and Origin of the Expression: An Englishman's Home is His Castle', www.phrases.org.uk, accessed 3 July 2019.

Famous men who worked as janitors

The editors of Encyclopaedia Britannica, 'Jim Carrey', Encyclopaedia Britannica, last updated 13 January 2019, www.britannica.com/biography/Jim-Carrey, accessed 3 July 2019; Ludovic Hunter-Tilney, 'Jon Bon Jovi on Hard Work, Losing His Wingman and US Inequality', 13 January 2017, *Financial Times*, www.ft.com/content/a3951c6c-d788-11e6-944b-e7eb37a6aa8e, accessed 3 July 2019; The Aberdeen Museum of History, 'A Walking Tour of Kurt Cobain's Aberdeen', www.aberdeen-museum.org/kurt.htm, accessed 20 July 2019; the editors of the Encyclopaedia Britannica, 'Stephen King', Encyclopaedia Britannica, last updated 6 February 2019, www.britannica.com/biography/Stephen-King, accessed 3 July 2019.

Environmental Performance Index

Environmental Performance Index, '2018 EPI Results', https://epi.envirocenter.yale.edu/2018/report/category/hlt, accessed 3 July 2019.

Dishwasher detergent

Suzy Strutner, 'Homemade Dishwasher Detergent Is a Real Thing, We Tried It', *Huffington Post*, 11 April 2019, www.huffingtonpost.com.au/2014/11/03/diy-dishwasher-soap_n_6087290.html.

Maria Telkes

Lemelson – Massachusetts Institute of Technology, 'Maria Telkes', https://lemelson.mit.edu/resources/maria-telkes, accessed 3 July 2019.

The most expensive house in the world
'Step Inside the 10 Most Expensive Homes in the World (including one in India)', Architectural Digest, 2 August 2018, www.architecturaldigest.in/content/worlds-most-expensive-home-india/#s-cust0, accessed 3 July 2019.

Coober Pedy
Coober Pedy Retail, Business and Tourism Association, 'About Coober Pedy', www.cooberpedy.com/about-coober-pedy-2/, accessed 3 July 2019.

The origins of spring cleaning
Gregory McNamee, 'Spring Cleaning and Its Origins', Encyclopaedia Britannica Blog, http://blogs.britannica.com/2008/04/spring-cleaning, accessed 3 July 2019.

Kashan door knockers
Lonely Planet, 'Kashani Door Knockers', www.lonelyplanet.com/iran/kashan/in-location/sights/e083d912-97c1-4895-b30a-853000ae0482/a/nar/e083d912-97c1-4895-b30a-853000ae0482/361014, accessed 3 July 2019.

WD-40
Readers Digest, '46 Amazing Uses for WD-40', www.rd.com/home/cleaning-organizing/13-amazing-uses-for-wd-40/, accessed 3 July 2019.

Eight: Children's Wingdings

Chinese birthdays
Naeun Kim, 'What is Age Reckoning?', SBS Online, 23 June 2016, www.sbs.com.au/topics/life/culture/article/2016/06/23/what-age-reckoning, accessed 4 July 2019.

The birthday paradox
Better Explained, 'Understanding the Birthday Paradox',
https://betterexplained.com/articles/understanding-the-birthday-
paradox/, accessed 4 July 2019.

George A. Kessler
Gare Maritime, 'The Champagne King, The Playwright and the
Savoy Hotel', www.garemaritime.com/the-champagne-king-the-
playwright-and-the-savoy-hotel/, accessed 4 July 2019.

Birthstones
International Gem Society, 'Birthstone Chart', www.gemsociety.
org/article/birthstone-chart/, accessed 4 July 2019.

Winnie the Pooh
Canadian Broadcasting Corporation, '90 Weird and Wonderful
Facts about Winnie the Pooh', www.cbc.ca/books/90-weird-and-
wonderful-facts-about-winnie-the-pooh-1.4089859, accessed 4 July
2019.

Nine: Mothers' Secret Business

North Pole, Alaska
Santa Claus House, 'Santa Claus House, North Pole, Alaska',
www.santaclaushouse.com, accessed 4 July 2019; Travel Alaska,
'North Pole', www.travelalaska.com/Destinations/Communities/
North-Pole.aspx, accessed 4 July 2019.

NORAD
NORAD, 'NORAD Tracks Santa', www.noradsanta.org/, accessed
4 July 2019.

Ten: School Daze

World's oldest educational institution

'Oldest higher-learning institution, oldest university', Guinness World Records, www.guinnessworldrecords.com/world-records/ oldest-university, accessed 4 July 2019; Fez Guide Advisor, www. fez-guide.com, accessed 22 July 2019.

Institut Le Rosey

Institut le Rosey, 'Welcome to Le Rosey', www.rosey.ch, accessed 5 July 2019; Millington, A. and Gorman, A., 'An Exclusive Look Inside the World's Most Expensive School, Where Tuition Fees Are Almost $150,000 a Year', Business Insider Australia, 29 June 2017, www.businessinsider.com.au/inside-the-most-expensive-school-in-the-world-2017-6#/#this-is-the-main-campus-of-institut-le-rosey-the-most-expensive-school-in-the-world-it-is-located-in-rolle-half-way-between-geneva-and-lausanne-on-a-28-hectare-estate-1, accessed 5 July 2019.

Peng Liyuan

Forbes magazine website, '#65 Peng Liyuan', www.forbes.com/ profile/peng-liyuan/#5426472f4fa4, accessed 5 July 2019.

Alice Springs School of the Air

Alice Springs School of the Air, 'Alice Springs School of the Air', www.assoa.nt.edu.au, accessed 5 July 2019.

One-room schools

North America: One-room Schoolhouse Center, 'Schoolhouses Still in Operation', http://oneroomschoolhousecenter.weebly.com/ still-in-operation.html, accessed 24 July 2019; **Maine:** Brianna Soukup, 'One Year in a One-Room Schoolhouse', *Lewiston Sun Journal*, 30 June 2019, www.sunjournal.com/2019/06/30/

one-year-in-a-one-room-schoolhouse/, accessed 24 July 2019; **Russia:** Facts and Details.com, 'Schools in Russia', http://factsanddetails.com/russia/Education_Health_Transportation_Energy/sub9_6a/entry-5142.html, accessed 24 July 2019; **Scotland:** Severin Carrell, 'North Ronaldsay: School with No Pupils Highlights Plight of Isolated Islands, *The Guardian*, 28 July 2017, www.theguardian.com/uk-news/2017/jul/28/north-ronaldsay-school-no-pupils-plight-of-isolated-islanders, accessed 24 July 2019.

School days around the world
National Center for Educational Statistics, 'Education Indicators: An International Perspective', www.nces.ed.gov/pubs/eiip/eiipid24.asp, accessed 5 July 2019; Organisation for Economic Co-operation and Development (OECD), 'How Much Time Do Students Spend in the Classroom?' in *Education at a Glance 2014: OECD Indicators*, 2014, www.oecd.org/education/EAG2014-Indicator%20D1%20(eng).pdf, accessed 5 July 2019.

World Teachers' Day
International Labour Organization (ILO), 'World Teachers' Day', www.ilo.org/sector/activities/sectoral-meetings/WCMS_646023/lang--en/index.htm, accessed 5 July 2019.

Left- or right-handed?
World Atlas, 'What Percentage Of The World Population Are Left Handed?', www.worldatlas.com/articles/what-percentage-of-the-world-population-are-left-handed.html, accessed 5 July 2019.

Finland education

www.smithsonianmag.com

Hancock, L., 'Why Are Finland's Schools Successful?', Smithsonian, September 2011, www.smithsonianmag.com/innovation/why-are-finlands-schools-successful-49859555/ www.smithsonianmag.com/innovation/why-are-finlands-schools-successful-49859555/, accessed 5 July 2019.

OECD Better Life Index

www.oecdbetterlifeindex.org/topics/education/.

Italian school holidays

School Holidays Europe, 'When Are the School Holidays in Europe?', www.schoolholidayseurope.eu, accessed 5 July 2019.

Maria Montessori

The editors of the Encyclopaedia Britannica, 'Maria Montessori', last updated 2 May 2019, Encyclopaedia Britannica, www.britannica.com/biography/Maria-Montessori, accessed 5 July 2019.

Acknowledgements

Thanks to Team Groff (family and friends who put up with my 'need to be alone' writer's nonsense), to Barry Brown for his laundry advice (that'll have tongues wagging at the golf club, Bazza), and to all folk mentioned in the research notes. Thanks also to all at Penguin Random House Australia who helped nurture this book to fruition, especially my publisher Sophie Ambrose, my editor Genevieve Buzo, and Louisa Maggio for her cover and design.

I must also thank Brian Dennis and Linda Anthony for their work behind the scenes, which brings me to my most special thanks which must go to my literary agent Selwa Anthony, who has been my guiding light in this game of words for over twenty years. Selwa, you are a honey of a human being and I couldn't have done any of it without you.

Discover a
new favourite